Books by Edith Patterson Meyer

DYNAMITE AND PEACE
The Story of Alfred Nobel

CHAMPIONS OF PEACE
Winners of the Nobel Peace Prize

PIRATE QUEEN
*The Story of Ireland's Grania O'Malley
in the Days of Queen Elizabeth*

THE FRIENDLY FRONTIER
The Story of the Canadian-American Border

MEET THE FUTURE
*People and Ideas in the Libraries
of Today and Tomorrow*

CHAMPIONS OF THE FOUR FREEDOMS

THAT REMARKABLE MAN
Justice Oliver Wendell Holmes

That Remarkable Man

Justice Oliver Wendell Holmes

Oliver Wendell Holmes at the time
of his graduation from Harvard in 1861

That

Remarkable

Man

Justice Oliver Wendell Holmes

by

Edith Patterson Meyer

BOSTON   Little, Brown and Company   TORONTO

FIRST EDITION

The author and the publishers wish to thank the proprietors for their
courtesy in allowing us to use the following illustrations:

Frontispiece, Harvard University.
Pages 19, 43, and 57, from *Justice Holmes: The Shaping Years, 1841–1870,*
by Mark De Wolfe Howe, Cambridge, Mass., Harvard University Press,
copyright 1957 by the President and Fellows of Harvard College.
Page 25, from *Touched with Fire,* edited by Mark De Wolfe Howe, copy-
right 1946 by the President and Fellows of Harvard College.
Page 61, from *Justice Holmes: The Proving Years, 1870–1882,* by Mark
De Wolfe Howe, Cambridge, Mass., Harvard University Press, copyright
1963 by the President and Fellows of Harvard College.
Page 89, the estate of Dr. and Mrs. Thomas Barbour.
Page 99, Macmillan and Company, London.
Page 103, The Library of Congress.
Pages 106 and 165, Harris & Ewing.
Page 168, from a portrait by Eben F. Comins.

Published simultaneously in Canada
by Little, Brown & Company (Canada) Limited

PRINTED IN THE UNITED STATES OF AMERICA

To my brother Herbert
in affection, admiration, and appreciation

Contents

That Remarkable Man
Justice Oliver Wendell Holmes

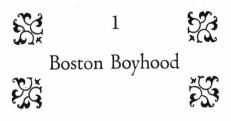

1

Boston Boyhood

AT THE END of a short street in the very heart of Boston stood the comfortable three-storied brick house where Oliver Wendell Holmes, Jr., was born. It was a quiet, rather secluded spot, yet from it you could go in minutes almost anywhere you might want to go. A short walk in one direction took Dr. Oliver Wendell Holmes, Sr., to the Harvard Medical School, where he taught anatomy. A short walk in the opposite direction took Oliver Wendell Holmes, Jr. — Wendell, he was called — to school. He first went to a little neighborhood "dame" school, then to Mr. Sullivan's school in the basement of the nearby Park Street Church. In 1851, at the age of ten, he started in at Mr. Epes Dixwell's new Latin School on Boylston Place.

Between home and Mr. Dixwell's Latin School stretched Boston Common — a wonderful place to play. Along with the other boys of the neighborhood — Cousin John Morse and the Cabot, Lodge, Eliot, and Wadsworth boys — Wendell slid down its steep grassy slopes, played marbles on its open spaces and hide-and-seek behind its great trees. In winter the boys raced their sleds down the Common's Long Coast and staged snowball battles against the Irish "toughies" who sometimes came up from the South End of the city looking for trouble. More than once Wendell's firm snowballs, which flew like arrows to the exact spot he wanted them to hit, turned the tide and brought victory over the intruding "Irishers."

When the Frog Pond in the Common was partly but not solidly frozen, the boys "ran tiddledies" on it. This meant getting to the other side and back by jumping from one piece of ice to another. It was ticklish business. A boy could not hesitate on an ice block; if he did, it would sink under him.

As soon as the ice and snow started to melt, the boys would run pell-mell down the narrow cobble-stoned streets to Boston Harbor to see the paddle-wheeled steamboats leave the docks for their first trip of the season across the bay. And from that time on Wendell, along with the other boys, kept an eye on the flagpole in front of the State House at the top of the Common to see when one of the sleek Boston-owned clippers was coming into the harbor. They could tell from the flag run up on the pole which ship was heading down the bay. If it was owned by the father of someone they knew, there was a good chance they would be allowed on board. There they would see weather-beaten sailors back from ports halfway around the world and hear stories of strange places and perhaps go home with some trifle from a far-off land or a foreign stamp or two.

Once a year Wendell could be sure of going to the circus when it spread its great tents on the Common for Mr. Barnum, its owner, always sent his father complimentary tickets. Dr. Holmes enjoyed taking Wendell and his younger sister and brother, Amelia and Ned, to watch the dancing horses and see the sideshows. He, too, liked going, for he was always interested in seeing people and especially in meeting those who knew him. Besides going with his father and Amelia and Ned, Wendell sometimes joined the other boys to follow the elephants as they were led to the Frog Pond to drink.

But Wendell did not need the excitement of a snowbattle, or running tiddledies, or boarding a clipper ship, or going to the circus. He was content to sit for hours curled up on the short flight of steps which led from near the front of his house on this dead-end street down into the street below. Sometimes he just watched the carriages and wagons and passersby, and sometimes he read to himself or aloud to Amelia and Ned. The house was full of books, for Dr. Holmes was a literary as well as a medical man.

Among Wendell's favorites were the stories of adventure written by Cooper and Scott and Melville.

Wendell liked to talk as well as to read, and he had a chance to do this at breakfast and at teatime — that is, if his father did not get started first. All the Holmes family liked to talk, Dr. Holmes most of all. He particularly liked to tell jokes and make puns. Some of these did not strike Wendell as being funny at all. Then he would not laugh politely, like the rest of the family, but just sit in silence. He showed his annoyance, too, when his father jumped in and finished a sentence for him if he hesitated a little when telling something that interested him. His mother, in her easy, gracious way, often helped him get going again. This never seemed to happen to Amelia or Ned. Ned was quieter, but Amelia was a chatterbox who kept on talking whether anyone listened or not. She was named for her mother, and Dr. Holmes liked to call them "Big A and Little A." The Holmeses' dining-room table, their friends and relatives agreed, was the "talkingest" place in all Boston. To encourage his children to express themselves well, Dr. Holmes offered a second helping of marmalade to the one who made the brightest remark at breakfast.

Wendell thought his father was hard to please and he worried because his father did not seem to have the same confidence in him and in his ability that his mother had. As Dr. Holmes's reputation grew until he became known as one of Boston's most famous citizens, Wendell felt increasingly ill at ease with him. Yet he was proud of his father's popularity as a lecturer, proud that he had studied medicine in Europe and was one of the few really scientifically trained men in Boston, proud of his father's intensive scientific research proving that infection was carried from bed to bed by physicians' unsanitary habits, and that he had saved the lives of thousands of young mothers by his insistence on changing careless hospital ways. Proud, too, of his father's courage in battling the bitter medical opposition his investigations aroused.

But Wendell wondered how a man so talented in medical matters could be so fond of cracking jokes, making gay verses, and writing long poems to recite at all sorts of Boston celebrations. And why was it that he took such pleasure in listening to people's praise of his verses and stories? Serious-minded Wendell puzzled over this; it was something he never could understand.

Across the Charles River in Cambridge, a short ride away by horsecar, Dr. Holmes's brother John lived with his aged mother in the old gambrel-roofed homestead. Wendell loved his spirited grandmother, who had outlived by many years her preacher-historian husband, and he felt very close to his easy-going, even-tempered bachelor uncle. Uncle John always seemed to understand how he felt about things; he sensed what was worrying him and said exactly the right thing to unpuzzle his mind.

In the summers the Holmes family often vacationed beside the sea in a quiet place a few miles north of Boston. Wendell loved scrambling over the granite rocks, wandering along the beaches, swimming and rowing and fishing at the edge of the ocean. Years later he remembered what fun it had been to fish from a dory anchored close to a little ledge where the motion of the water made the seaweed hanging from the broken barnacles swing back and forth.

For several summers the family went to the Berkshires, the hilly section of western Massachusetts, where Dr. Holmes built a summer home on property owned long before by Judge Wendell, Grandmother Holmes's father. It was glorious vacation country. From Canoe Meadow, as they called their place, they could see the peak of lofty Greylock and the meandering Housatonic River, and smell the scent of the pines and of sun on fields of clover and new-mown hay.

The three Holmes children roamed over the fields and woods, climbed trees, went blueberrying, fishing, and exploring. Wendell had a perch in a tall pine, where he liked to curl up with a book. If, looking down, he saw one of the more interesting neighbors — perhaps Longfellow or Hawthorne or Melville — coming to call, he would slide down and linger at the edge of the group, listening intently to their good talk. He was always glad when Grandmother Holmes and Uncle John came to join the family, as they sometimes did for weeks at a time. One year the Holmeses, except for the Doctor, had an extra two months in the Berkshires because yellow fever had broken out in Boston. Dr. Holmes stayed in the city, working hard to help fight the epidemic.

Every fall, after the family returned to Boston, there were Saturday outings. Dr. Holmes owned three boats which he kept moored on the Charles River just beyond the far edge of the Common. Wendell often used the dory to row across to his grandmother's house or to explore the banks of the Charles far above the city, or to fish beneath an overhanging shady bough.

During the long winter evenings there were games and books and conversation before the hearth fires, with many friends dropping in. Wendell did not share his father's deep interest in science, although he made a few efforts in that direction. Once he sat for hours bent over one of his father's microscopes, examining and carefully drawing some strange little things that he saw in the liquid in the jar beneath it. He was sure that he had discovered something important, but when he showed his drawing to his father he was told that the strange specks were nothing more than air bubbles.

Dr. Holmes loved the theater, and so did Wendell. He looked forward in winter to the Saturday matinees to which his father sometimes took him. Even more exciting were the times when on a quiet evening the fire whistles would suddenly blow and Dr. Holmes would spring up, head for the door, pulling on his coat and shouting, "Come on, Wendell!" Down the street they would go in a mad dash after the prancing firehorses and the smoke-bellowing red fire-engine. This happened fairly often, for at that time there were many wooden buildings even in the heart of Boston.

At twelve, Wendell was a sturdy, alert, intelligent boy, fond both of books and of fun. People commented on his high forehead and steady blue-gray eyes, and that he was tall for his age — taller, in fact, than his somewhat undersized father. This was something that Wendell was keenly aware of — and so, he knew, was his father. It was a subject better not mentioned.

In the 1850's the problem of slavery was causing much concern all over the nation, even in New England. Bostonians had a great respect for property; they also believed firmly in the rights of the individual. These two beliefs clashed violently when an escaped slave from the South appeared in their city. Was he, as the Southerners claimed, a piece of property to be returned to its owner? Or was he a human being, with the right to freedom? The talk was heated, and opinion was divided. For days the Negro was held in the courthouse jail only a few blocks from the Holmeses'. Wendell, like everyone else, waited breathlessly for the judge's decision. The Abolitionists, who believed that slavery should be ended at once and forever, held fiery meetings in Faneuil Hall. Most respectable Bostonians considered their views radical and did not go along with them, at least not all the way. Some people were afraid that if the slaves were freed they might flood into the North and take over the jobs in the cotton mills that were helping to make Boston prosperous. Many agreed with the politicians who were trying to balance Northern and Southern interests and keep things on an even keel. They felt that the Government was doing a smart thing in admitting states to the Union in pairs — one state where slaveholding was legal for every one where it was not.

Wendell's feelings were mixed. He wanted the jailed Negro slave to be free, yet he did not approve of the radical Abolitionists breaking into the jail to try to free him, and he was glad that law and order won out over the riot they caused. But he was sorry to have the slave returned to jail and sorrier yet when he learned the next day that, as the Abolitionists had feared, the judge had decreed that the slave was the property of his Southern master and must go back to him. At dawn the dark-skinned man was led through the Boston streets under heavy guard and put aboard a ship in the harbor for his return to the South and slavery.

Wendell thought a good deal about this. It turned him toward the side of the Abolitionists to the point where, years later, he said, "In my youth I was an Abolitionist and shuddered at a Negro minstrel show, as belittling a suffering race, and I am glad that I was and did."

Studies went on at Mr. Dixwell's Latin School — Latin, Greek, French, and a smattering of mathematics and of ancient history. Wendell did fairly well, though not brilliantly. School work came easily to him, and he did not take his studies too seriously. His many friends and outside activities interested him more.

One rather unusual hobby of his was a somewhat neglected form of art — etching. As a small boy he had seen, among other marvels in the rooms of one of the early China merchants, an engraving which had impressed him so much that he used to dream about it. Then his father gave him some portfolios of engravings and etchings he had bought when he was a student in Paris. Wendell pored over them, fascinated by their expressive thin lines and amazing detail. He began to haunt book and art shops, looking for old folios and prints. In the Boston Athenaeum, the fine private library to which his family belonged, he read books about etchings and etchers. He practically memorized the descriptions in a dictionary of engravers, until he could recognize a large number of prints when he saw them. With his limited pocket money he managed to pick up "one or two good things and more rubbish." Among the good things were a few Dürer woodcuts. Because of the long and careful consideration he gave each one, these purchases brought him more joy than if they had come easier. He bought a set of etching tools and tried his skill at the art. Perhaps he was overcritical of himself; anyway, he decided that his work was poor and gave it up. But all his life he kept his appreciation of etchings and engravings and his fondness for collecting them.

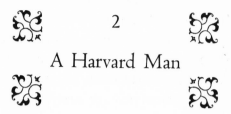

2

A Harvard Man

MANY OF THE BOYS at Mr. Dixwell's Latin School planned to go to Harvard. This was not only because it was generally considered the finest college in the country, or because it was just across the river in Cambridge. It was, most of all, because going to Harvard was in the best Boston tradition and was definitely "the thing to do." For Wendell Holmes, Harvard was taken for granted. It was also taken for granted that he would enter at sixteen, for this had become a sort of habit in the Holmes family — something that father, uncles, and cousins all had done.

To his relief, Wendell made it. He did not have the best grades in the world, but he finished the Latin School with the blessing of its head, Epes Dixwell, with the affectionate cheers of Amelia and Ned, with the reassuring confidence of his mother, and with the demanding requirements of his father.

And so, in the autumn of 1857, Oliver Wendell Holmes, Jr., became "a Harvard man."

Dr. Holmes made arrangements for his son to room in a private house just off the College Yard. Like the other students who lived there, Wendell Holmes was expected to leave his bed at six in the morning and return to it at nine in the evening. After dressing in his cold and rather cheerless room he hurried out for breakfast and then made his way on through the often uninspiring routine of the long day. Classes, he was disappointed to find, were not very different from those at Mr. Dixwell's Latin School. No one had a chance to choose the subjects he was especially interested in. The four hundred or so students all took the same courses, memorized passages from the same textbooks, listened to the same lectures — often dry as dust — and plodded through the frequent written exercises. And then grumbled like schoolboys at the marks the professors gave them.

The real zest of college, Wendell decided, came from the friends one made and from the outside activities, such as skating on the Charles, hiking over to Boston with a bunch of the fellows for a supper of oysters and beer, battling in the annual sophomore-freshman fracas in the Yard, or going for tea and talk with Uncle John and Grandmother Holmes in the big house so close at hand. Or calling on Fanny

Dixwell, daughter of his former schoolmaster, to enjoy her lively conversation and her talent, so rare in the Holmes family, for listening. Like Uncle John, Fanny seemed really to appreciate his stories and his attempts at philosophizing. She made him feel good, and confident that he would someday amount to something in the world — as much, even, as his father. His mother had told him this, but he found it hard to believe.

Besides the boys from the Dixwell School there were other Boston boys whom Wendell knew in his class at Harvard, but he found it more exciting to meet and make friends with those from farther away. Norwood Penrose Hallowell, a pleasant boy from a Philadelphia Quaker family, soon became one of his best friends.

During his freshman year Wendell spent his weekends with his family in Boston. After that, he was not allowed to go home so often. Home was in a different place now, for business houses and stores had crowded in so close to the quiet little street on which Wendell had grown up that Dr. Holmes had decided to move. He bought a new house on Charles Street. There was a broad outlook onto the river from the back of the house, and from his third-floor room Wendell could see across to Cambridge and the hills beyond. At first it seemed strange to visit his family in this new place, but he soon grew accustomed to it.

Dr. Holmes was disappointed with his son's grades at Harvard. In his second year Wendell was barely in the first third of his class — scarcely a good showing for a Holmes. But the Doctor was glad to see that his eldest son had inherited some of the Holmes writing ability. An essay of his on books and reading was printed in the *Harvard Magazine*. In it young Holmes expressed his conviction that a person should read what he liked instead of what was considered to be "the thing" to read. This year also (in true O.W.H., Sr., manner) he wrote a set of verses for the sophomore banquet.

Of a sudden Wendell developed a great interest in the Greek philosopher Plato. He dug into the subject and for Christmas asked his family for an English translation of Plato's works, published in London. When the books arrived he studied them carefully and was amazed to find in them so much "modern" thinking. During his six-week winter holiday he wrote down his reactions, planning to submit the paper in the annual Harvard undergraduate essay contest. Before turning it in, he decided to ask a real authority to read and criticize it. A little hesitantly he showed the essay to the noted philosopher he called "Uncle Waldo" — Ralph Waldo Emerson, one of his father's good friends.

Emerson read it carefully, while Wendell fidgeted on a chair nearby. Slowly the great man shook his head. "When you strike at a king, you must kill him," he said.

For a while after this Wendell did not have the heart to do anything with Plato. Then, meeting Emerson one day, he was surprised when the philosopher encouraged him to "give Plato another chance." It took months, off and on, to write his paper, but it was time well spent. Not only did it win the next year's prize in the undergraduate essay contest, but it was published in the *University Quarterly*. Most important, this study of Plato introduced Wendell Holmes to the satisfactions of painstaking research and philosophical pondering. He never underestimated Emerson's influence in this, and called him "the firebrand of my youth."

Harvard freshmen and sophomores were not admitted to college social organizations, but as a junior and senior Wendell Holmes belonged to several clubs, including the Hasty Pudding and the Porcellian. He was good company, fun-loving but not boisterous, ready for a lark but seldom getting himself into troublesome tangles. To his father's delight his grades improved so much in his last two years that he "made" the honor society, Phi Beta Kappa. He also became editor of the *Harvard Magazine* and wrote several articles for it, including one on the

Oliver Wendell Holmes, Jr.,
as an undergraduate at Harvard

work of Albrecht Dürer, the German artist whose woodcuts and etchings he admired so much.

Slavery was a subject much discussed at Harvard. There were many Southerners in the college; their ideas differed from those of most Northerners. Neither did all Northerners think alike; there were many different shades of opinion among them. Some of Wendell's friends were strong Abolitionists. He was not as radical as many of them but he believed in the cause enough to go over to Boston to help protect Wendell Phillips and other Abolitionist speakers from coming to harm at the Anti-Slavery Society meetings. Feeling ran so high that mobs threatened to beat up the speakers after they left the hall, and sometimes actually did so. Lincoln's election stirred up more feeling in Boston and Cambridge, but it was not until the "cotton states" seceded that people's eyes were opened to the very real possibility of war between the North and the South.

The Massachusetts Home Guard called for volunteers, and in the Boston State House the Governor ordered rifles and overcoats for the state militia. When Fort Sumter was fired on the month after Lincoln's inauguration and the President called for seventy-five thousand militia, the Massachusetts Governor was the first to respond. Within a week, trained and equipped troops headed South from Boston.

Before the end of that month of April, 1861, Wendell Holmes had joined the New England Guard, along with Norwood Hallowell and several other college friends. Dressed in dark blue tunics over light blue baggy pants tucked into gaiters, and with red sashes and red caps, the Home Guard sailed down Boston Bay to Fort Independence. There they were to drill and to watch for the possible appearance of armed Southern privateers. None of these showed up, but each Sunday families and friends, including attractive young ladies, arrived in numbers, bearing baskets of goodies for their brave soldier boys.

The Harvard seniors in the Home Guard might still graduate, the college authorities decreed, provided they returned and passed their final examinations in June. Hallowell was to be the class orator and Holmes the class poet on Class Day. The poem was written at Fort Independence, between periods of drilling and guarding. Back in Cambridge, the two friends, clad in academic gowns, marched together toward the church on the big day, and Wendell expressed the hope that his rhyming would not be so poor as to distress his father who, he knew, was sure to be in the front row with the rest of the family.

And so he was, but everything went off well, and Dr. Holmes actually beamed at his tall son. The ordeal over, Wendell relaxed and gladly joined the gala crowd in the College Yard, where there were cool drinks and ices. After that, Dr. Holmes had arranged to have a "spread" served for the family and special friends in his son's room.

In the late afternoon people flocked back to the Yard, where there was music, and soon the young people were dancing. Pretty, vivacious Amelia, seventeen now, was besieged by young men. Fanny Dixwell, too, was surrounded by admirers. Wendell noticed almost for the first time how good-looking she was, and how popular. At the end of the dance came the traditional ceremony, with the students forming rings around the class tree — freshmen outside, then sophomores, juniors, and on the inside ring the eighty seniors. Hands joined, they moved slowly around the tree, singing "Auld Lang Syne." Wendell felt a lump in his throat as he wondered vaguely what might — or might not — lie ahead.

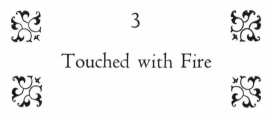

3
Touched with Fire

THE NEXT FEW YEARS were a far cry from that festive ring around the class tree in Harvard's College Yard. To Wendell Holmes the Civil War was "a crusade in the cause of the whole civilized world," and a personal challenge which he could meet only by taking part in it. Many of his classmates felt as he did. Forty-seven of them fought for the Union, many of them giving their lives.

"Through our great good fortune, in our youth our hearts were touched with fire," Wendell Holmes said later. "Touched with fire" he was indeed — physically, mentally, and spiritually. For three awful years he lived his faith, putting love of country and loyalty to an ideal above personal safety, comfort, and ambition. In the midst of the horrors of war, the sudden death of close friends and the likelihood of his own, he worked out his philosophy of life. It was to accept doubts and disillusionments and an imperfect universe where struggle was natural; to sink his personality into something greater than himself; to find pleasure in duty; to respect honor, courage, and his fellow men, including his foes ("every man with a heart must respect those who give all for their belief") ; to consider life "a profound and passionate thing," and to find joy in living it.

Holmes received his commission as lieutenant in the Twentieth Massachusetts Regiment in July, 1861, and was ordered to a training camp a few miles out of Boston. From there, because recruiting was going slowly and he was a good talker, he was sent to the Berkshires to try to interest the youths of western Massachusetts in joining the army. In this region where he had spent many of his boyhood summers he was welcomed by old family friends and by new young-lady acquaintances. They liked this tall, "spare" young man with the friendly smile and the pleasant voice. And a little girl of nine was so completely enamored of this "erect, manly boy of twenty" and he so enjoyed her company that, through occasional letters, cards, and calls, the friendship continued for seventy years.

By September, Lieutenant Holmes was back with his regiment, ready to travel to Washington with it by wagon, boat, and train. After camping first on Georgetown Heights, then on Meridian Heights within sight of the unfinished Capitol, the Twen-

Oliver Wendell Holmes in Civil War uniform. This undated
photograph was probably taken in 1861 when Holmes was training as a private in the Fourth Battalion

tieth marched to a point near Harper's Ferry. There the soldiers set up their tents on the northern bank of the Potomac and began regular drilling and guard and picket duty. They could hear the drums of the "Secesh" on the other side of the river but were forbidden to fire across. It was an exciting way to live, Wendell Holmes wrote his family, but "I long for letters — write all of you all the time."

The Twentieth's first engagement, at Ball's Bluff, was mismanaged and disastrous for the Union soldiers. Lietuenant Holmes was calm as the noise of cannon became deafening and bullets whizzed around him like hail. He was proud that the men he led showed no fear, even as the enemy forced them back over the corpse-littered ground toward the cliffs of the Potomac.

A spent bullet mowed him down and knocked the wind out of him, but after a moment he was up and crawling back to the front. This time it was a live bullet that hit him, entering his left chest, and missing his heart by half an inch. Comrades, crisscrossing arms to make a chair, carried him unconscious down the cliff. All about them men were dying, dropping into the river, or swimming and struggling to get the wounded into the pitifully small number of available boats. Bullets flew overhead as they crossed to an island in midstream. A surgeon who took a look at Holmes in a makeshift shelter thought the wound fatal, but he turned him over to let it drain and gave him an opiate before going on to the next wounded man. Holmes's men carried him across the island in a blanket and ferried him to the Maryland shore. A painful ride over rough roads in a jolting two-wheeled cart brought him to a field hospital at dawn. To everyone's surprise, and to his own, after two days he had recovered enough to be able to scratch a few lines to his family. With satisfaction he wrote about the battle, "I felt and acted very cool and did my duty I am sure."

A week later Lieutenant Holmes traveled to the Hallowell home in Philadelphia and from there his father took him to Boston on a stretcher. The Doctor, rejoicing over his son's "most narrow escape from instant death," was full of questions, but Wendell was silent. At first he slept a good deal and would not talk of the battle at all. Then he began to read, to look at his portfolios of etchings, and to entertain callers. "Wendell is a great pet," the Doctor wrote a friend, noting especially the number of young ladies who came to call on the wounded war hero. By the end of the year young Holmes was able to walk, and not long after he was ordered to travel about the state recruiting, in an effort to fill up the ranks of the Twentieth after its heavy losses at Ball's Bluff. In March, a captain now, he returned to his regiment.

As part of the Army of the Potomac, the men of the Twentieth suffered the misery of the heartbreaking Peninsula Campaign. Day after day they plodded through foot-deep mud in shivery cold and driving spring rains, bent on taking the Confederate capital of Richmond. They were hungry and thirsty, dirty, covered with lice, sick with dysentery, sleeping at night unsheltered, in wet uniforms. Yet they marched on, firing and fired upon by the unseen enemy which lurked behind hills, in cornfields and woods. Holmes and his men grew accustomed to the sight of fields full of dead bodies, to pools of blood, and to the heartrending cries of dying soldiers.

"We go forward," he wrote his family, "passing a deserted battery the dead lying thick round it and then begins the deuce of a time." He bragged that though one regiment broke there was "not a waver in our Reg." Often he drew little pen sketches or diagrams to illustrate his letters. His family was not to worry, but please would they write oftener!

Throughout the agony of the unsuccessful Virginia Peninsula Campaign the Massachusetts Twentieth set a record for bravery — and for heavy losses. Years later Holmes claimed that "the Twentieth was a regiment that never talked much about itself but that stood in the first half-dozen of all the regiments of the North for number of killed and wounded in its ranks."

Still Lee held Richmond. The Twentieth was moved across the river now, into friendlier Maryland. In mid-September came the battle of Antietam. Once again the Union Army was forced to retreat and casualties were heavy. For Holmes it was another "most narrow escape from instant death." In Boston a telegram awakened the Holmes household in the middle of the night: CAPTAIN HOLMES WOUNDED SHOT THROUGH THE NECK THOUGHT NOT MORTAL AT KEEDYSVILLE.

The next day Dr. Holmes was on his way South, along with several other Boston fathers bent on the same errand. They traveled in silence. For perhaps the first time in his life the loquacious Dr. Holmes did not feel like talking. With his sure knowledge of the body's anatomy he pictured the veins and arteries of the neck and calculated the slim chances of a bullet passing harmlessly among them.

He stopped at the Hallowells' in Philadelphia and found the two soldier sons at home, one with a shattered arm, the other delirious with typhoid, but no news of Captain Holmes. On the Doctor traveled, to Frederick and on to Keedysville. There he learned that the Captain had left for Hagerstown the day before, in a milkcart. His son must be heading for Philadelphia, the Doctor reasoned, so he went back to the Hallowells'. But Wendell was not there and they had had no word of or from him. Once again the anxious father took off, traveling to Harrisburg, through which Wendell must pass to go from Hagerstown to Philadelphia by rail. All along the way Dr. Holmes followed every clue, searched in the hospitals hastily set up in churches and schools, inquired through every possible channel for news of his son. At last, in Harrisburg, he had an answer to one of his frantic telegrams. Captain Holmes was in Hagerstown, "doing well," and was leaving the next morning for Harrisburg. For the first time in more than a week, Dr. Holmes relaxed. He had a good night's sleep and in the morning boarded the train from Hagerstown bound for Philadelphia.

Near the front of the first car sat the object of his search. No show of emotion now, he warned himself; Wendell doesn't like that. According to Dr. Holmes's story, published in the December, 1862, *Atlantic Monthly,* the greetings exchanged were "How are you, Boy?" and "How are you, Dad?" This, Holmes, Jr., said was fiction. Never had his father called him "Boy," and never had he called his father "Dad." But though the greetings were unemotional, the meeting was a welcome one. Wendell explained rather unconvincingly his five-day stay in Hagerstown in the home of friendly strangers, then lapsed into silence. The physician father looked at the closed eyes, the bandaged neck, the thin body — and kept silent, too.

After a night's stopover with the Hallowells in Philadelphia and another at a New York hotel, the father and son went on to Boston and home, where Wendell, affectionately welcomed, was put to bed in his own room. There he remained, well cared for but withdrawn. How could he talk and be gay when all he could think of were the awful battlefields, the dead friends, the sights and sounds of dying men? For some weeks he could not raise his left arm, but gradually this condition improved, as did the rigidity of his neck.

Dr. Holmes's obvious pleasure in the success of his widely read *Atlantic* article, "My Hunt after 'the Captain,'" was not shared by his son. He thought the story far too personal and sentimental and an unpardonable invasion of his privacy. Yet he had to admit that the detailed description of a countryside devastated by war, of the movement of a retreating army, even of a battlefield visited only hours after a battle were both graphic and accurate. Though he cringed at it, he had to admire this evidence of his father's keen powers of observation and of his writing ability.

Once again came the difficult leavetaking from the family and the return to the front. A veteran soldier of twenty-one — and feeling twice that age — Holmes rejoined the Twentieth at its winter quarters on the Rappahannock. Almost at once he was hospitalized with dysentery. He wept, he admitted later, at not being able to lead his men in the unsuccessful attack on Fredericksburg. The spirits of the men in the Union Army were low; they were deserting by hundreds. Captain Holmes did not waver in his belief that slavery must be ended and the Union held together, but he did begin to doubt that these aims could be accomplished by force — at least by the force of the Union Army as he saw it.

In the advance against Chancellorsville Holmes was hit for the third time. A bullet struck his heel with an impact so great that it tore ligament and tendons and splintered the bone. Again came a period of convalescence in the Charles Street home, with the attending Boston doctor cleverly using a raw carrot to plug the wound yet keep it open. With skillful care both the danger of losing the foot and the fear of permanent lameness disappeared, but the wound healed slowly. There was time for reading books of philosophy and sociology, and for thinking, and for long, serious talks with a few special friends. News came of the three-day battle at Gettysburg, with the Southern forces turned back but not defeated, and with more close friends killed. Those were sad days for Wendell Holmes.

As soon as he was able, he went out around the state to recruit more men for the Union Army. In Boston, Dr. Holmes wrote and spoke for the Union cause, and Mrs. Holmes and Amelia worked weary hours at the Commission which helped organize, train, and equip hospital units.

At the beginning of 1864, orders arrived for Captain Holmes. He was assigned to the Sixth Corps staff headquarters, with a sort of honorary rank of lieutenant colonel. No longer would he lead his company into action. Instead, he would serve as field officer, carrying dispatches between generals, sharing their tensions and uncertainties as new lines of defense were set up.

In the early spring the Union Army went into action. General Grant was now its head, but still it fought on with no real success. Holmes confided to his diary and sometimes in letters that he had "hardly known what a good night's sleep was since the campaign opened"; that "bullets are now whistling round these H.Q."; that "the whole ground stunk horribly with dead men and horses of previous fight"; that it was hard even to remember home as a reality; and that "if one didn't believe this war was a crusade, in the cause of the whole civilized world, it would be hard indeed to keep the hand to the sword."

Washington was threatened and Grant sent three brigades to Fort Steven to defend it. Holmes was there with General Wright when President Lincoln came to see the Union troops throw back the attacking force. When the President climbed the parapet to get a better view of the battle, General Wright advised him to move, but he did not. Men fell from enemy bullets as he stood there, an easy target with his great height accentuated by his tall hat.

Shouting, "Get down, you fool, before you get shot!" Wendell Holmes rushed to grab the tall man. He spoke with no regard for rank and acted with such vehemence and authority that the President obediently stepped down. Before he left the battlefield President Lincoln turned back to speak to the soldier who had probably saved his life. "I am glad you know how to speak to a civilian, Captain," he is reported to have said.

The Southern troops drew back, and Washington was saved. "So far all right — fighting every day," Holmes wrote his family. And he related his narrowest escape of running into about twenty enemy soldiers when carrying an important dispatch one night, of disregarding their "Halt! Surrender!" and of running the gauntlet lying along the neck of his horse. "Got my dispatch through and return in triumph to find myself given over for lost," he ended. "Love to all Afftly OWH, Jr."

Captain Holmes wondered how much longer he could endure the dangers and hardships and exhaustion of this life. In May he wrote his parents that "these nearly two weeks have contained all of fatigue and horror that the war can furnish. . . . nearly every Regimental off I knew or cared for is dead or wounded. . . . I think there is a kind of heroism in the endurance of the men. I tell you many a man has gone crazy since this campaign begun from the terrible pressure on mind and body. . . . I hope to pull through but don't know yet — Goodbye — Afftly, OWH, Jr."

At last he made up his mind that if he lived until his three-year term was up he would not reenlist. "Prepare for a startler," he wrote home. "Unless something unexpected happens, I shall probably leave this army for home about the 17th! The Reg. ceases to exist as a Reg and the few old men not reenlisted leave for home to be mustered out."

As the train carried him northward, Holmes's thoughts were on his dead comrades, on his three years of fighting for his ideal of freedom — to end slavery and to hold the nation together, while the South fought just as valiantly for its ideal of freedom — the right to pull apart and live in its own way as a separate nation.

"Captain Holmes," a war correspondent reported, "served more than two years steadily and chivalrously as a line officer, was three times severely wounded, and in this campaign has been zealous and indefatigable as a member of the Sixth Corps staff, has always been conspicuously daring, and capably efficient, and he goes out of service because his regiment does, not because he would taste the sweets of home and Boston."

Holmes' own comment was brief. "I started in this thing a boy. I am now a man."

The impact of the Civil War on Holmes was evident all his life. Again and again that war was clearly in his mind as he stated a belief with telling force. "It is for us to fix our eyes upon the point to be stormed, and to get there if we can." . . . "I think that, as life is action and passion, it is required of a man that he should share the passion and action of his time at peril of being judged not to have lived." . . . "Let a person have nothing to do for his country and he will not care for it."

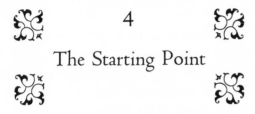

4
The Starting Point

"IF I SURVIVE the war I expect to study law as my profession, or at least for a starting point," Wendell Holmes had written in his biographical sketch for the Class Album just before his graduation from Harvard. Was that only three years before? It seemed like thirty! Well, decided Captain Holmes, the law was probably as good a starting point as any other.

When he informed his family that in September he would enter Harvard Law School Mrs. Holmes and Amelia were pleased. So was Ned, who was beginning his second year at Harvard that fall. But Dr. Holmes, who had once started to study law and then, hating it, had switched to medicine, snorted, "Law! A lawyer can't be a great man."

Stubbornly Wendell Holmes held to his decision, realizing at twenty-three the truth of what he said later, "No one can direct the life of another man. . . . Each has to work out his own way."

His war wounds still bothered him as he rode the jolting horsecars to Cambridge and carried home heavy books to pore over in the evening. But he persisted, reading into the history and philosophy of the law far more deeply than the law professors required, and often talking over legal problems with young lawyer friends in his pleasant third-floor sitting-bedroom after dinner.

Was the law concerned only with tradition and with details that would narrow a man's mind — as his father insisted? Was it worthy of the interest of an intelligent man? He must find out for himself. If the law could not extend his horizons; if he could not "live greatly" in the law, he wanted no part of it.

Before deciding on law school, Holmes had considered studying philosophy, perhaps going on to teach the subject in a college. He had even talked about this with "Uncle Waldo" Emerson. Holmes recognized himself as an "internal" kind of man. He knew that ideas meant more to him than things, and philosophy, he believed, "opens the vista of the farthest stretch of human thought." But he decided that a career in philosophy was not very practical. He also decided that in taking up law he would not have to give up his interest in philosophy, because "the law will furnish philosophic food to philosophic minds." Since law was part of the whole scheme of things it surely could reveal as much of the universe as any other part — "if you have the eyes."

Holmes joined the Harvard law students' club, named for the great Supreme Court Justice John Marshall. The mock cases put on by the club provided a more practical and far livelier approach to the profession than did the classroom lectures. Each man took his turn at presenting cases and at judging the arguments. Twice Holmes presided as judge over the pretended courtroom.

After a winter of studying law Holmes was still a bit uncertain about his choice of profession, though he would never have admitted this to his father. But by summer he could write to a friend, "I think my first year at law satisfies me. Certainly it far exceeds my expectations." By the next school year he was sure. "Law, of which I once doubted," he wrote, "is now my enthusiastic pursuit. I am up to my ears in it all the time."

This was not quite accurate. The young law student found time for freqent visits with his companionable bachelor Uncle John, who had lived alone since his mother's death at ninety-three; time for evenings with William and Henry James and other young men friends; time for social evenings with personable young ladies, and especially time for excursions and parties with Fanny Dixwell. She was sweet, smart, and fun to be with, and a much better listener than was anyone in his family — and Wendell did love to talk.

When news finally came of the end of the long, bloody war, Wendell Holmes felt a sense of personal relief. No more pangs of conscience now about re-enlisting! Like the rest of the country he was shocked at President Lincoln's assassination and he feared what might happen to the war-exhausted nation, but he had no interest in taking an active part in politics. He was finding the study of law, particularly its history and underlying philosophy, absorbing.

That summer of '65, after his first year at law school, the Holmes family had a cottage at the beach at Nahant, not far from Boston. So did the Dixwells. Wendell spent some time at Nahant; he also joined Henry James for a vacation in the White Mountains. There a gay group of young people climbed mountains and had good times together. Once, when they were setting out on a day-long expedition, Wendell insisted on taking along a little girl who begged to go with them. Throughout the day he devoted himself to giving her a good time, telling her stories as they walked and staying with her when the rest of the party climbed too high for her. She made him think of that other little girl with whom he had struck up a gay friendship when he was recruiting in the Berkshires two years before.

It was still not unusual, though not quite so common as it had been in the days before law schools, for a young man who intended to become a lawyer to study in the office of an established attorney. In exchange for the use of law books and the practical knowledge gained from seeing the preparation and handling of actual cases, the young man made himself useful copying wills and other documents, going on errands to the courthouse or to other lawyers' offices, and looking up legal points and precedents in law libraries.

During the fall term of Holmes's second year at Harvard Law School he had a chance to combine this sort of experience with his formal study. Mr. Robert Morse, a Boston lawyer with a good practice, invited him to spend his afternoons in the Morse law office. Young Holmes found copying deeds and wills deadly dull, but he enjoyed watching Mr. Morse and his associates in action and gained a new insight into the practice of law.

While Wendell Holmes was in his last term at law school William James was a medical student at Harvard. The two friends saw a good deal of each other, often talking late into the night on weighty, unanswerable questions involving the universe and man's relation to it. "Twisting the tail of the cosmos," they called these philosophical conversations. Like Holmes, James was an "internal" man, to whom ideas were more interesting and important than things.

Before Holmes finished his law course in May, 1866, he was invited by George Shattuck, a fine lawyer and a fine man, to come into the Chandler, Shattuck and Thayer law office in the fall to read for his bar examination. This was the hurdle that must be leaped before becoming a practicing lawyer. With the Shattuck association set up, Holmes could let himself become excited over the trip to England which his family was giving him that summer. Dr. Holmes secured letters of introduction to some of the people his son especially wanted to meet, including the sociologist John Stuart Mill and Thomas Hughes, author of *Tom Brown's School Days*. Wendell also anticipated meeting Frederick Pollock, an eminent judge, and Leslie Stephen, a literary man and member of a famous legal family, whom he had come to know on a visit Stephen had made to Boston.

England was all young Holmes had anticipated — and more. His eager appreciation of both London landmarks and the English countryside, his easy acceptance of English customs and courtesies, and his gay friendliness made him a welcome guest. Invited to some places because of his father's name, he soon became a favorite in his own right — which was much more to his liking. Once, when someone in-

Oliver Wendell Holmes, 1866

quired if he were the son of Oliver Wendell Holmes the poet, he replied, "No, he is my father."

He was often in the home of Charles Francis Adams, the American minister to the Court of St. James's, and was invited to social affairs with the minister's daughter Mary and his son Henry, who was acting as secretary to his father. John Stuart Mill took Holmes to the Political Economy Club to dine and listen to a discussion; afterward they walked about the London streets, talking together earnestly. In the Chancery Court of Lincoln's Inn, so Holmes wrote home, Lord Chancellor Pollock "called me up and had me sit beside him, which I did until the adjournment. People looked at me and grinned."

He saw Stratford and Oxford and was entertained at country estates where he watched cricket and went boating on the Thames and had his fill of formal dinners and teas. He flirted with beautiful women and in a letter home complained of one gathering, "No one pretty there." In Scotland he spent a day in Edinburgh and was a guest of the Duke of Argyll. Everywhere he enjoyed himself. He felt at home with the traditions, attitudes, and tastes of the English. Yet he commented that though class consciousness was lessening, the upper classes were "still a good way off from the simple human basis on which an unspoiled American meets you."

A hurried trip to the Continent took Holmes first

to Paris, where he visited the galleries and walked beside the Seine, then on to Switzerland, where he climbed the Alps with his English friend Leslie Stephen and Stephen's brother. Their fourteen-hour expedition "almost recalled an army march" and left him burned, stiff, and exhausted, but with unforgettable memories of the finest views he had ever seen.

Back in Boston, Holmes happily shared his summer's memories with his family, then reported at the Chandler, Shattuck and Thayer office to begin his preparation for admission to the bar. Two attorneys, duly appointed to this task, would examine him orally and no one could predict what sort of questions they might ask.

George Shattuck, Holmes's sponsor, was just the man to prepare him for the ordeal. An extremely able trial lawyer, he could think fast and well on his feet and he was filled with enthusiasm for his cases. Chandler, the senior member of the firm, was a slow-moving, conservative lawyer of the old school. Thayer, the most scholarly of the three, had his heart set on a law professorship at Harvard.

Holmes was nervous about the examination; he was also nervous about the whole business of becoming a practicing lawyer. He knew he had the brains for the law but he doubted if he had the temperament. His taste still ran to philosophy rather than to practical details. But he took to heart Shattuck's words that to become a first-rate lawyer one must at some period immerse himself in the law completely, for "the business of a lawyer is to know law."

Holmes read with a sort of fierce determination, not only the books in the law office but weighty tomes from the nearby Boston Athenaeum. Evening after evening he read and studied in his room. No matter how difficult or dreary the book, he did not skip. "If a man chooses a profession he cannot forever content himself with picking out the plums but must eat his way manfully through crust and crumb," he wrote his friend William James, who was now studying in Germany. In addition to his reading, Holmes made abstracts from legal records of related cases for Mr. Shattuck's use, and he frequently visited the county courthouse as Mr. Shattuck's aide or as an observer.

In November, two friends of Holmes's started a magazine which they named the *American Law Review*. It was to cover developments in both American and English law, and they invited Wendell Holmes to review recent law books for it. This was a task exactly to his liking. It gave him a chance to read the latest law books and, in return for his review, to keep them. His reviews were thoughtful and thorough. He seemed to have a knack for getting at the heart of a subject and for writing about it clearly and forcefully. With some pride he showed his mother his first review, printed in the January, 1867, *American Law Review*. Her constant faith in him and her certainty that he would one day be as great as his father encouraged him in his deep urge to succeed. He felt the need to "live greatly," but in his own way and outside the shadow of his father.

By February, Wendell Holmes decided that he was as ready to take the bar examination as he would ever be. The necessary petition was filed and Mr. Shattuck's letter of recommendation sent in. The date was set for early the next month.

On the big day Holmes sat across a desk from his two examiners. Nervous at first, he soon became calm and easily answered the few questions they put to him. He breathed a tremendous sigh of relief as he realized that the ordeal he had dreaded was over. Within a few days he returned to the courthouse to be sworn in as a practicing lawyer of the Commonwealth of Massachusetts. After the ceremony he signed the register of members admitted to the bar, paid five dollars for his certificate, and went back to his desk in the Chandler, Shattuck, and Thayer law office. To celebrate the occasion he bought himself a new chair and ordered a card to be printed: OLIVER WENDELL HOLMES, JR., COUNSELLOR AT LAW.

His work with the firm went on much as before. Prompted by his ever-ready sense of humor, he penciled a note during a nasty snow-and-sleet storm

a few days after his certification: "The rush of
clients postponed on account of weather." More
relaxed with the bar examination behind him, he let
up a little on his heavy reading schedule. One
Sabbath Day that spring he took over his sister
Amelia's Sunday School class and delighted the children by reading to them Hans Christian Andersen's
story of "The Ugly Duckling." When summer came
he went to Maine for two weeks of fishing and also
joined Henry James and other friends in the White
Mountains for a few days of climbing.

By now Holmes had become a really valuable
assistant to Mr. Shattuck. He still did not enjoy the
work of preparing cases and sometimes agreed with
his father's idea that law was largely made up of
details. "A ragbag from which they [lawyers] pick
out the piece of the color they want," he said. In
November, as Shattuck's Junior Counsel, he argued
a case in court — and lost. He had worked hard on
it, conscientiously looking up precedents, piecing
together known facts, making logical deductions.
But it had not interested him particularly, and his
family thought he did not seem very upset at losing
the case.

He had put off writing a long overdue letter to
William James in Germany until Fanny Dixwell
coaxed him into it. Now he wrote his friend Bill that
his life held little but "law — law — law." It was

true. During the day he slaved at his job as Junior Counsel to George Shattuck. Evenings he read books on law and wrote reviews and articles for the *American Law Review*. He was a better critic and writer on law than he was a practicing lawyer, and he knew it. He was developing a brilliant style, easy to read and often with a touch of dry humor in it.

As he went on working with Mr. Shattuck and handling the few petty cases that came to him personally, Holmes became depressed. Time was slipping away, and here was he, creeping up toward thirty and still not a success or even the beginning of one. He was not even completely financially independent, and he still lived at home. To be sure, he was most welcome there. Money was no problem in the Holmes family. Mrs. Holmes's father had left quite an estate, and Dr. Holmes had a good income from his lecturing and writing and from fortunate investments.

In a long letter to Bill James that next spring, Wendell Holmes claimed that since December he had "worked at nothing but the law." Still, he said, he counted "the long grind of the winter" a success, both for "the simple discipline of the work" and because he was sure now that a person could keep his ideals in the study and practice of law. He had a good deal to say about the coming of spring. "The icy teeth have melted out of the air and winter has snapped at us for the last time." But in a postscript he added, "It is snowing again. S'help me."

When Bill James returned from Europe he and Holmes spent nearly every Saturday evening together. James called Holmes's devotion to his work appalling, but he wrote his brother Harry, "I think he [Holmes] improves surely every year, and has that in him which makes you sure his fire won't burn out before the age of thirty as 'most everyone else's seems to."

That summer of 1868, Wendell Holmes and Henry Cabot Lodge, then a student at Harvard, went West — all the way to Illinois — to shoot prairie chickens. Someone warned them about rattlesnakes, so they wore thick boots and, said Holmes, "jumped a yard on the prairie every time a cricket stirred in the grass." They shot some prairie chickens but did not see a single snake.

Refreshing vacations, pleasant companionships, lively conversations, good food and wine, girls — who seemed to like him as much as he liked them — happily filled Wendell Holmes's spare hours. These things were all fine for relaxation, he thought, or to bring new insights into life, but ahead of them he put work. He was, as one of his friends said, "composed of at least two-and-a-half different people rolled into one." For he loved both life and law — provided it was the scholarly, not the humdrum, side of the law.

5

Fanny at Last—and Kent

FANNY DIXWELL was far too high-spirited and proud to let Wendell Holmes see how much she thought of him. Mrs. Holmes noticed but kept silent though she hoped, for she liked Fanny and thought her just right for Wendell. Ned openly told his older brother that he wasn't very discerning about Fanny. Wendell paid no attention. Bill James called Fanny "the best girl I have known. . . . She is A1, if anyone ever was." And he admitted that he would like to be the man — the only man — in her heart but knew that Wendell Holmes had first place.

Wendell Holmes liked girls and enjoyed the pleasant game of flirting with them. But it never occurred to him to flirt with Fanny, though he liked her best of all. She seemed almost like family to him, and he took her pretty much for granted. Ever since his freshman year at Harvard, except when he was away at war, he had been dropping in at the lively Dixwell home in Cambridge once or twice a week, maybe oftener. They all knew it was Fanny, the oldest daughter, he came to see. She would go boating, skating, or on a picnic with him at a moment's notice, and he could depend on her always being good company. When anything important or interesting happened to him Fanny was the first one he told about it. He liked to be with her, but he felt he must keep his mind on the law and get ahead in this profession he had chosen. "If you haven't cut your name on the door of fame by the time you've reached forty, you might just as well put up your jackknife," he said — and firmly believed it. Yet here at nearly thirty he had hardly made a scratch!

His chance came when Mr. Thayer, the third member of the firm he was associated with, was invited to edit the twelfth edition of Kent's *Commentaries on American Law*. It was a big job, involving a good deal of research in both American and English law records. American lawyers depended on "Kent," as they called the commentaries, for accurate information on matters of common law. Mr. Thayer, being busy with other legal activities, asked Holmes to help, and presently turned the whole task over to him.

Wendell Holmes soon saw the necessity for a complete overhauling of the editions which had come out in the twenty years since Kent's death. He wondered how the amount of work he felt was needed could ever be done in the two years allowed for the preparation of this new edition. Yet he was determined to make this a superlative job, a real contribution to legal literature. Law books, the tools of the profession, were pitifully inadequate, as every practicing lawyer knew.

Holmes worked on the job practically every waking hour outside of his law-office duties. He became more and more absorbed in the task. This was the kind of law work he loved — the history and development of the law and the philosophy that lay behind it. He wanted these commentaries not only to provide specific information but also to point up the changing nature of law as well as its continuity over the centuries.

Wrapped up in Kent, Holmes had little time for his family, his friends, even for Fanny. One evening he did interrupt his work long enough to dine with the James family and afterward Mrs. James wrote her son Harry of her concern about Wendell. "His whole life, soul and body, is utterly absorbed in his *last* work upon his Kent. He carries about his manuscript in his green bag and never loses sight of it for a moment. . . . His pallid face, and this fearful grip upon his work, makes him a melancholy sight."

In the fall of 1870, the Holmes family moved from the house on Charles Street to a new brownstone Dr. Holmes had built farther out, on the extension of

Beacon Street which had been filled in from the Back Bay marshes. Wendell, absorbed in his Kent, hardly noticed the move. As in the old house, both his room and Ned's were on the third floor, looking out across the river toward Cambridge. As before, most of his evenings were spent on the growing pages of the Kent manscript. Every night before retiring he took the green bag (the usual color of the heavy cloth book bag used by lawyers before the days of briefcases) downstairs and placed it beside the front door. It must be the first thing to be carried to safety in case of fire, he informed the household.

That fall Holmes left the Chandler, Shattuck and Thayer office to set up the Holmes and Holmes law firm with Ned. This younger brother had finished Harvard Law School with flying colors and was now a promising young lawyer, ready and able to carry the greater share of the work of the new law firm. Wendell meant to do his part, but his heart was really on the Kent job, and on two other assignments that had come to him.

He had been invited by Charles Eliot, the new president of Harvard, to lecture on constitutional law at the college. Though his rank was only that of instructor, it was a real opportunity and one that fitted in neatly with the research he was doing for the Kent. Already he had used some of his findings in an article for the *American Law Review,* with the result that he was asked to become a co-editor of the magazine, along with Arthur Sedgwick. Part of his duties would be to produce more articles, book reviews, and editorials — which he would enjoy doing if only there were more hours in the day. That fall, too, he argued a case in county court for the firm of Holmes and Holmes and won it. This did not surprise Arthur Sedgwick, who declared that Holmes "knows more law than anyone in Boston in our time, and works harder at it than anyone." Between Kent, the magazine, the lectures, and the law firm, it was true that Wendell Holmes's life held practically nothing but "law — law — law."

His life might have gone on this way but for the drastic actions of a few members of the Holmes family. In 1871, both Amelia and Ned Holmes married, leaving only Dr. and Mrs. Holmes and their eldest son in the big Beacon Street house. Wendell became more than ever conscious of being the son of the family, still to a degree financially dependent on his father. He felt like a small boy when his father called, as he always did when he saw his son heading for the door, "Where are you going, Wendell?"

Ned, Wendell knew, had nothing to worry about; he had a canny sense of stocks and bonds and such things and he had married a wealthy woman. The small income Wendell had from his Harvard instructorship, from the Holmes and Holmes law firm, and from the law magazine was scarcely enough to live on. Occasionally this situation bothered him and bothered him very much. Yet when his mind was occupied with matters of the law, as it was so much of the time, he gave little thought to the problems of his personal life.

It took observant, understanding Uncle John to change the situation. Getting along in years, still unmarried but wise as ever, he took Wendell aside one evening and talked to him like the proverbial Dutch uncle. How long was it since he had seen Fanny? Had he looked closely at her lately — noticed how pale and drooping this once high-spirited girl had become? And had he asked himself the reason? Didn't he have eyes in his head to see that the girl was in love with him, was pining away for him? And didn't he realize that he was in love with her?

Wendell was shocked, stunned. No, he had not realized any of this. But once his eyes were opened, he let no grass grow under his feet. Within hours he was calling on Fanny; within days they were making plans for their wedding.

They were married in June by Dr. Phillips Brooks in Boston's Christ Church — the only church, Fanny quipped, big enough to hold all Wendell's old girl friends. For a brief honeymoon Wendell left behind the familiar green bag bulging

Fanny Dixwell, 1868

with Kent material. Then, for reasons of practical convenience and financial necessity, the newlyweds settled into the third floor of the Holmeses' residence. Fanny made it into a cozy home, and when Wendell's or her friends called they were entertained upstairs in the Junior Holmeses' own sitting room.

Both Dr. and Mrs. Holmes were enormously fond of Fanny and delighted to have her with them. She listened better than did Amelia to Dr. Holmes's chatter and to the letters of extravagant praise from admirers of his books and poems which he loved to read aloud. She entered with enthusiasm into Mrs. Holmes's household and social activities and set up her own for herself and for Wendell. Yet she did not try to slow down her husband's intellectual pace — much. She saw to it that after the evening meal he could escape to his third-floor lair and his waiting work without wasting valuable time socializing with his parents and their many guests. She encouraged him by listening attentively to the articles he wrote for the *American Law Review* (he did one within a month of their marriage) and to his plans for his law class at Harvard. She was intelligent about her remarks, for she had read more than one book of law while patiently waiting for Wendell to wake up to his feelings for her and hers for him.

Wendell Holmes enjoyed his teaching and was

pleased that his class was popular. Instead of dull lectures on legal theories and precedents, he held the interest of his students by talking to them informally and by encouraging them to ask, "Why?" and to analyze the reasons behind the principles of law. Sometimes he turned the classroom into a court, in the manner of the John Marshall Club, from which he had learned so much when he was a Harvard Law School student. A committee appointed to visit college classes visited his — and approved, even adding that they had no suggestions to make.

At home Fanny helped lessen the frequent tension between father and son by quickly changing the subject or by relating something amusing she had seen or heard during the day. But she could see that the natures of father and son were poles apart, and that Wendell's talents would never fully develop while he was living under his father's roof. Yet until he became more securely established in his profession this arrangement seemed necessary. Perhaps, she hoped, when the Kent was finished?

In spite of its editor's diligence, preparation of the twelfth edition of the Kent *Commentaries* took a year longer than the two-year period allotted it. At last all four volumes were finished and at the printers. The first winter after their marriage Fanny helped her husband read proof on them, and the next spring Kent was published. The reviews came in slowly. Wendell and Fanny Holmes read them eagerly and were pleased that they were nearly all favorable. "The thirty-two-year-old editor is a lawyer of extraordinary gifts," one reviewer said. Another mentioned the scholarly and painstaking work he had done in collecting and sifting a great mass of legal material. Still another commented that the editor had "moved with the new currents of law and legal thought." Clearly, in editing the Kent, Wendell Holmes had achieved his "ambition of excellence."

Only Mr. Thayer seemed displeased. Originally it had been agreed that both his name and Holmes's should appear on the title page. When Holmes took over the entire job and went so much further with his research than there had been any idea of at first, he felt entitled to take complete credit for the work, and so his name stood alone on the title page. Even though Mr. Thayer might have seen the justice of this he did not like it, and he called Holmes a self-centered and ambitious man, thoughtless of others. This did not much bother Holmes, but it bothered his wife considerably.

After a short vacation to celebrate the publication of Kent, the third-floor study lamp again burned late as Wendell prepared to finish up the year's law class, and read and review law books and write a few articles and editorials for the *American Law Re-*

Oliver Wendell Holmes, Jr., 1872

view. He was giving up his magazine editorship and the law class at Harvard, after three years of "lectureships." He felt that Fanny deserved something better than the kind of life these part-time occupations could provide, and the chance had come to give it to her.

George Shattuck was forming a new firm, and he had invited Wendell Holmes to join it. Ned Holmes was quite capable, his brother knew, of going on with the Holmes firm alone. When Wendell protested to Mr. Shattuck that he was no good at the business end of things, Mr. Shattuck replied that he did not need a business-getter but a man who was a thinker and who knew law. The third member of the firm was to be William Munroe, a quiet, industrious, friendly fellow a couple of years younger than Holmes and a competent lawyer. Holmes considered George Shattuck a "dear and intimate friend," one who had taught him much and had done him many kindnesses. This offer was still another kindness for, as Mr. Shattuck hinted, the young Holmeses could certainly find uses for the money the new connection would bring. Holmes knew that with Shattuck at the helm, the firm of Shattuck, Holmes and Munroe was sure to succeed.

The practice of law was not any more to Wendell Holmes's liking now than before, but he worked at it conscientiously, Mr. Shattuck seemed satisfied, and

Fanny was pleased. That fall Mr. Shattuck made it possible for the couple to acquire a little shore place near his own on Buzzards Bay, where they could spend weekends and vacations by themselves or have their friends come to see them. They got along on very little, economizing in many ways, such as using a small cart drawn by a bit of rope to haul the dirt they needed to raise a few vegetables and the flowers of which Fanny was so fond. The wheelbarrow they eventually bought — a major investment — paid off, and Bill James coming to see them, reported finding Wendell "stooped over his little plants."

The following summer Wendell Holmes was able to fulfill his deep desire to return to England and to introduce his wife to English life and to his English friends. It was a wonderful summer for him. He threw off his Boston reserve, seeming to Fanny a little like his father in his thorough enjoyment of garden parties, teas, and dinners. Frederick Pollock, the young lawyer who was to become Wendell Holmes's lifelong friend and correspondent (son of the judge who had invited young Holmes to sit beside him on the bench on his earlier trip to England), described Holmes's accomplishments as a conversationalist: "He would catch a subject, toss it into the air, make it dance and play a hundred tricks, and bring it to solid earth again. . . . Talk was a means of clarifying ideas, of moving toward the truth; but it was a great game too."

Unlike her brilliant husband, Fanny was tongue-tied and miserable. In large gatherings she was overcome by shyness. Only when they were safely in their room would her usually quick tongue loosen. There she commented acidly on the "twinkling hippopotamuses" at the party, those "fat old ladies with immense bosoms and larger stomachs, both adorned with gold and precious stones." Gradually she persuaded her husband to go alone to luncheons, dinners, and parties. Her taste, she explained, ran to simpler things, such as visiting quietly with a few friends, or exploring the fascinating streets and byways of London and collecting perfume bottles. The English countryside she enjoyed, but she would take Boston to London any day. Even their third-floor rooms in the Beacon Street home seemed like heaven to her after their return in September.

Soon, however, Fanny found a little flat for them to move into. It was over a drugstore on the second floor of a remodeled building at 10 Beacon Street, right next to the Athenaeum and convenient to Holmes's office and the courts. The two rooms were sunny and pleasant — and cheap. No new furniture was needed. Pine boxes would serve nicely as book-cases for Wendell's law books. Breakfast could be cooked on a gas plate; other meals they would have to eat out, sometimes at the nearby Parker House, where the food was excellent and they were sure to meet congenial friends.

Now at last the Junior Holmeses had a touch of the independence they both craved and needed. Their lives were their own, with no one to question their comings and goings. They would run out, hand in hand, to follow the fire engines to a fire like happy children bent on adventure. They took turns reading aloud to each other until all hours of the night. Often Fanny knitted or concentrated on her special kind of needlework — original tapestrylike pictures done in worsteds on a silk background — while Wendell worked on cases for the office or, more happily, on articles for the law magazine. He had taken to doing more of these as he found that, besides bringing in extra funds, they provided a sort of release from the routine of the office and an outlet for the part of his brain seldom used in the daily practice of law.

Looking at her husband, Fanny realized that he was growing handsomer every year. Wherever they went, his erect, soldierly figure, the lean aristocratic lines of his intelligent face lighted up by his sparkling gray-blue eyes and accented with the flowing mustache he cultivated, attracted attention—especially from the ladies. Fanny liked to tease him about this, not minding at all that he enjoyed their admiration, because she knew beyond doubt his deep devotion to her and hers to him. Their quiet, almost frugal life might lack luxuries and excitement, but it was rich in companionship, understanding, and love.

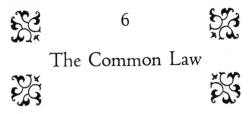

6

The Common Law

THE TIME LIMIT Wendell Holmes had set to make his mark in the world was getting close. His teaching at Harvard, his writings for the *American Law Review,* and his editing of Kent had brought him favorable recognition but not renown. And his work as a practicing lawyer with the firm of Shattuck, Holmes and Munroe had been adequate but had not added much to his reputation. All in all, up to this point, his accomplishments were not enough to satisfy his ambition. And it was no comfort to him to see his father, now in his seventies, still gaily accumulating honors, fame, and fortune.

Lawyer Holmes felt fretfully as if he were on a perpetual treadmill. He must practice law to make a living, even though he and Fanny both realized that his talents lay in the scholarly, not the practical, side of the law. If only he had money enough to devote his life to exploring the history of law and analyzing its principles! How he would love to write a book — a book that did not exist — to show the development of common, everyday law and explain why and how modern legal rules and procedures had grown out of earlier customs and why and how they had changed since those earlier days. "Doctrines," he said and firmly believed, "get swerved from their true meaning and extent because we do not remember their history and origin."

Most lawyers thought that modern law was chiefly rooted in the law of the ancient Romans. Henry Adams, now a lecturer at Harvard and a close friend ever since that first trip to England, had opened Holmes's eyes to the possibility that modern law might be even more deeply rooted in the customs of the old Germanic tribes. The idea interested Holmes so much that he took up the study of the German language so that he could read the German scholars in their own tongue and determine for himself just how and how much the Germans had influenced English — and so American — law.

Like Holmes, Adams belonged to "The Club," a group of men connected with Harvard who met together regularly to dine and to discuss matters of importance. Holmes was now a member of the Harvard Board of Overseers. Always devoted to his Alma Mater, this honor pleased him greatly.

Wendell and Fanny Holmes could have belonged

to almost any group in Boston and filled their life with dinners and parties, theaters and concerts. Instead, almost every evening found them in their little flat, seated beside the gas reading lamp, Fanny doing her embroidery or reading, Wendell poring over his heavy law books or writing scholarly articles for the *American Law Review*. His days belonged to Shattuck, Holmes and Munroe, but his evenings were his own, and these were what he lived for. Fanny would listen attentively as he read aloud what he had written. She would make some keen comment and perhaps suggest some slight change — which her husband nearly always considered an improvement.

Wendell Holmes's great chance came in 1880. Every winter for many years the Lowell Institute had offered a series of lectures which were attended by the more intellectually inclined Bostonians. The lecturers were carefully selected and were invited far enough ahead to give them plenty of time for the careful preparation of their material. Dr. Holmes had been a Lowell Institute lecturer one winter. Now his son, Oliver Wendell Holmes, Jr., was invited to give a series of twelve lectures on the law.

It would mean, Wendell explained to Fanny, giving over practically every evening for months to preparing the lectures. The *American Law Review* articles could form the basis of some of them, but there would have to be a good deal of new material, which he would have to dig out from old law books and records. The lectures must be carefully organized so that each subject would lead clearly and logically to the next. But, said Wendell happily, the twelve lectures taken together could also make a book — that badly needed book he had been longing to write. And there would be time — just barely time — for the book to be published by his fortieth birthday — his self-set deadline.

That summer and fall there were no vacations for the Holmeses, no visits, no going to concerts or the theater, no running to fires. It was not easy, as a letter to Pollock explained: "One gets ahead but slowly when his only chance is to sit down after dinner and after a day of more or less hard work." But by November, when the lecture series was scheduled to start, Oliver Wendell Holmes, Jr., was ready.

He called the course simply "The Common Law," and he began with a lecture on "Early Forms of Liability." Many people came to hear that first lecture — Boston lawyers, professors and law students from Harvard, personal friends and relatives, regular Lowell Institute attenders. Dr. and Mrs. Holmes were there, of course; Amelia, a widow now; Ned, a successful lawyer but in painfully poor health. Some came not because of interest in the law but out of curiosity to see how the tall son of the world-famous Boston poet would do.

He did all right. From the first sentence it was plain that he knew his subject like the back of his hand and also that he knew how to make it clear to others. His manner was informal and easy — almost as if he were talking with a group of friends in someone's parlor. He rarely looked at his notes; wherever possible he used everyday language instead of legal terms, and he punctuated his points with dozens of homely little examples which everyone could understand. For example, to illustrate the difference between harm done accidentally and intentionally he said, "Even a dog distinguishes between being stumbled over and being kicked."

His opening words made lawyers open their eyes. "The life of the law has not been logic; it has been experience." Law, Holmes went on, could not be dealt with like a book of mathematics, for "the law embodies the story of a nation's development through many centuries," and its rules are determined by "the felt necessities of the time" and even by the prejudices of the judges.

This was a totally new concept of the law. It startled some of the lawyers in the audience, trained to consider the law as eternal and unchanging. Were they supposed to believe that the law could and should change as society changes? That its very life ought to depend on its recognition of existing conditions? Yet they knew the truth of Holmes's statement that many a law remained in force "long after the causes which gave rise to it had disappeared." They followed with mounting interest his carefully developed explanation of the way in which changes in the law had come about and the way in which the pressures and demands of society had helped it to grow.

As Holmes peeled off layer after layer of formal phrases to show the fundamental principles beneath them, the more learned of his listeners realized that they were hearing something altogether new — an analysis of the law by a philosophic legal historian. They might object to some of his criticisms of certain legal practices, such as the different verdicts given by different courts in similar cases, which he termed "little better than lawlessness," but they had to concede that every point was logically and understandably argued.

The attendance did not fall off after the first lecture. A newspaper reported: "No other course in the Institute in recent years has been attended by so large a proportion of men — an evidence both of the interest they have in the law and the power of Mr. Holmes to interest them."

Every week, besides working on the next lecture, Holmes went over the last one, paring it down and polishing it for its appearance in printed form. He was determined that each paragraph should stand up not only on a first reading but for years to come.

Early in the new year the manuscript was ready for the printer, and only a few days before Holmes's fortieth birthday in March *The Common Law* came off the press. It was truly a stupendous accomplishment. In sending a copy to his friend Pollock Holmes wrote, "My heart has been deeply in it." He proudly presented an inscribed copy to his father. Here at last was clear evidence of his ability, "the achievement by which he wanted to be judged at the age of forty." Years later, when a friend asked if it was an original contribution, Holmes replied, "So far as I know I made the thread, wove the cloth, and cut the pattern."

The years of "grinding labor" and of withdrawal from society were rewarded. More quickly than after the Kent, the reviews came in. Even lawyers who did not agree with all of its conclusions respected the book. Its reviewers said that it had given "a powerful direction to legal science"; that it had "broken down walls of formalism and empty tradition"; that it was a "noble concept of a realistic and rationalized science of law." Lawyers pondered over its author's prediction: "The law has got to be stated over again; and I venture to say that in fifty years we shall have it in a form of which no man would have dreamed fifty years ago."

Harvard's President Eliot was not unaware of the stir Holmes's lectures and book were making in the legal world. He was not a man to overlook an opportunity to promote the interests of his college, and in the spring of 1882, he offered the author of *The Common Law* a full professorship at the Harvard Law School.

Holmes was delighted, and so was his wife. It seemed exactly the right place for him. He accepted gladly, though he heeded George Shattuck's warning to leave himself free in the unlikely event that a judgeship should be offered him. Twice there had been such openings and each time the Governor had appointed someone else. Still, at Shattuck's insistence Holmes wrote in his acceptance letter: "If a judgeship should be offered me, I should not wish to feel bound in honor not to consider it."

President Eliot agreed. After all, such a possibility was slight. The position of a Harvard Law School professor was a proud one; most professors stayed on for life — naturally. Mr. Holmes, President Eliot decreed, should begin his work in the fall, at the start of the college year.

The summer before taking up his new assignment Wendell and Fanny Holmes went again to England and also on a short trip to France, Germany, and

Switzerland. As before, Wendell enjoyed himself immensely, seeing old friends and making new ones, but Fanny was happiest when they were back in Boston.

Holmes started his teaching in late September. He kept his connection with the law firm though he put in little time there. Eager to make his law course exciting to the students, he worked from actual cases instead of assigning them a portion of a law textbook to study before each session. His students had never before used their brains so hard or learned so much. Holmes, it seemed, was a born teacher, well qualified to succeed in his aim to turn the Harvard law students into learned, thinking, open-minded lawyers.

The first term went ahead rapidly. Then toward the end of December came, as Holmes expressed it later, "a stroke of lightning which changed the whole course of my life."

One of the judges on the Massachusetts Supreme Court resigned, and the Massachusetts Governor decided to give Professor Holmes the vacant seat. First, however, he must have Holmes's consent to place his name before the Council, which must approve the appointment. The Governor asked George Shattuck to contact his partner. There was no time for deliberation; he must have an immediate answer.

George Shattuck picked up Fanny Holmes and

hurried over to Cambridge. There, outside Holmes's Harvard classroom, he broke the news to him. Taken by surprise, Holmes hesitated. He liked teaching. He liked being at Harvard. And he knew that President Eliot would not take kindly to his leaving.

Shattuck grew impatient. What did President Eliot's opinion matter? This was Holmes's big chance; he must not miss it.

Holmes thought fast. On the bench he would be in the thick of things as he never could be in the classroom, and "the place for a man who is complete in all his powers is in the fight." A judgeship would certainly "extend his range." Happy though he was at Harvard, if he turned down this opportunity he would probably always regret it. He could tell how Fanny felt just by looking at her, even though she insisted on leaving the decision entirely to him. She had once warned him not to limit his capacities by becoming too content in his professorship.

And so Professor Holmes authorized the Governor to present his name to the Council. After its approval he informed President Eliot of his decision and attended a faculty meeting where he explained, rather badly, why he was leaving. President Eliot called his resignation "a great blow to the Law School." The abrupt action also disturbed some of Holmes's colleagues, especially his old associate, Professor Thayer, who had been partly responsible for the professorship being set up and who did not know of the reservation Holmes had made in the acceptance of it. John Gray, Holmes's closest friend on the Law School faculty, was appointed by President Eliot to take over Holmes's course for the second term, but the students enrolled in it were sorely disappointed at losing their favorite professor.

Much later Holmes wrote his friend, law professor and jurist Felix Frankfurter, "Academic life is but half life — it is withdrawal from the fight." Whether he would have felt this way if he had not experienced the "stroke of lightning" no one will ever know. Perhaps in accepting the challenge offered him he anticipated the satisfaction it would give him to deliver from the bench perceptive opinions based on his years of study of the law and his intense desire that the law should deal out justice equally to all.

7

Massachusetts Judge

"WELL, I LIKE MY WORK far more than I dreamed beforehand," Judge Holmes wrote to his English friend Frederick Pollock the summer after his appointment to the Supreme Judicial Court of Massachusetts. "The experience is most varied — very different from that one gets at the bar, and I am satisfied most valuable for an all round view of the law. . . . One sees too a great deal of human nature, and I find that I am interested all the time."

In his early forties Oliver Wendell Holmes, Jr., had finally found his place in life. He brought to the judgeship an impressive knowledge of the law, enormous energy, and high ideals. The other six members of the bench, all older than Holmes, had been a little fearful of the appointment, but they soon discovered that the new judge was easy to work with, always courteous, and often stimulating. The Chief Justice assigned to him even more than his share of cases to write up, having observed that he listened attentively and got to the heart of a case with amazing speed. "The great thing is to have an eye for the essential . . . to try to strike the jugular and let the rest go," was Judge Holmes's motto. His opinions combined good law and good sense, with sometimes even a touch of humor.

Holmes did not find the seemingly unimportant, run-of-the-mill cases uninteresting. In some of them he uncovered points worth studying. "Law is human," he said emphatically; "it is part of man and of one world with all the rest." Lively or dull, he judged each case conscientiously, acting under a keen sense of public responsibility.

As a judge, Wendell Holmes was even more satisfied with his choice of the law as a career. "What a profession it is!" he exclaimed in a speech at a bar association dinner. "Every calling is great when greatly pursued. But what other gives such scope to realize the spontaneous energy of one's soul? In what other does one plunge so deep in the stream of life — so share its passions, its battles, its despair, its triumphs, both as witness and actor?" Holmes "had the same passionate interest in the law," an attorney observed, "which a great painter feels for art or a scientist for science."

Soon after Professor Holmes became Judge Holmes, he and his wife moved from their two-room flat to a house of their own, also on Beacon Hill. After they had looked at another house and jointly turned thumbs down on it, Mrs. Holmes had suggested, "Why not leave it to me?" The next the Judge heard about it was when she invited him to dine at No. 9 Chestnut Street. Once he approved the house, so the Judge said proudly, she sent him off to England for his vacation and spent the summer getting it in shape, "determining which should be my library and even the color of the shelves against the will of the architect and coming out clearly right."

It was a pleasant house, with room for some of the Dixwell and Holmes heirlooms and the wedding presents stored for so long. Favorite etchings found a place on the walls, and in a sunny room Fanny kept the caged birds that she loved and that were company for her when her husband was away. Part of his work was to conduct equity courts in Springfield or Pittsfield to the west or New Bedford to the south. Sometimes he was gone for as long as a fortnight; more often he got back to Boston for the weekends. With the salary of a judge, the Holmeses were able to employ a cook and a maid. They could eat their dinners at home now, and even share them with friends. They could have evening parties, with good conversation lasting till well after midnight, and an occasional overnight guest.

Fanny Holmes had never been so happy as in this, their first real home. Her husband loved to watch her feed and talk to her birds or work on her artistic embroidered panels. He was not alone in considering her an artist with her silks and satins and worsteds. Fourteen of her unusual embroidered nature scenes were exhibited in Boston one year and the following year in New York, where they were highly praised for their design and color combinations.

The year after Wendell Holmes became a judge talented Ned, long gravely ill with asthma and heart trouble, died. Uncle John, though lame and feeble, lived on in his Cambridge bachelor quarters, as interested as ever in everybody and everything. Mrs. Holmes, Sr., was growing frailer, but Dr. Holmes, well into his seventies, was still spry, taking his daily walks in the Common and continuing to dote on the attention he received from admiring readers of his articles and poems. He wrote regularly for the *Atlantic Monthly* and was also working on a biography of his friend Emerson, who had recently died.

When Judge Holmes was invited to make the 1884 Memorial Day speech in Keene, New Hampshire, his mother in her gentle way encouraged him to go. He should tell the people about his war experiences, she said, and how he felt about war and other important matters.

So the Judge went, and his wife went with him. In the big hall, decorated with flags and bunting and sweet with the scent of lilacs, sat row upon row of soldiers no longer young, clad in the blue uniforms of the Union Army, and behind them scores of Keene's townspeople. They looked up expectantly at the man standing tall and erect on the platform, the morning light playing on his heavy head of hair and his flowing mustache.

He would try to answer the question a young man had put to him: "Why do people still celebrate Memorial Day?" It is, said the Judge, the day on which we "pause to become conscious of our national life and to rejoice in it, to recall what our country has done for each of us, and to ask ourselves what we can do for our country in return." He said that to fight out a war "you must believe something and want something with all your might. So must you do to carry anything else to an end worth reaching. More than that, you must be willing to commit yourself to a course, perhaps a long and hard one, without being able to foresee exactly where you will come out. All that is required of you is that you should go somewhither as hard as ever you can. The rest belongs to fate." He related acts of heroism he had seen in the war and told of friends who had died nobly for their country. "It was given to us," he said gravely, "to learn at the outset that life is a profound and passionate thing."

It was a solemn, impressive speech which no one who heard ever forgot. The address did not go unnoticed in Boston, either, and from then on Judge Oliver Wendell Holmes, Jr., was asked to address many gatherings. He did not accept nearly all of the invitations that came to him, but from time to time he did speak at different Harvard functions, at law schools, at bar association events, and to pay tribute to deceased members of the bar. He spoke well, partly perhaps because he usually rehearsed his speech to his wife beforehand. But it was what he said much more than the way he said it that accounted for many of his speeches becoming classic examples of noble thinking, nobly expressed in beautiful, flowing prose.

Times were changing, both in Boston and in the rest of the country. Industry was replacing agriculture; city living was taking the place of rural life. Problems of labor and of unions, of capital and of giant corporations pressed in upon the work of the courts. Many of the judges had been brought up in a way which led them all-unconsciously to favor the side of capital and the employer. Holmes urged judges to guard against letting their personal prejudices influence their decisions. His own attitude was more detached, more impartial, and more tolerant than that of most of his associates. The importance placed on money and on power in this era of big business did not impress him at all. He believed that employers and employees had equal rights under the law.

More than most judges, Judge Holmes had the "creative insight to understand and interpret the New America that was growing up." He had the genius to look back into history and forward into the future and to see their connection. "Without the courage to change perpetually there is no growth," he said, "and without reverence for tradition there is human and social disaster." His understanding of social changes came from a sort of sixth sense. Unlike his friend Louis Brandeis, the Boston attorney he had known at Harvard Law School, he did not dutifully read the daily papers or investigate situations personally or consult authorities to gather facts on current affairs. Holmes admitted frankly that facts bored him. Yet he had an uncanny ability to get to the bottom of a subject while others were still pottering around the edges. This ability was credited to his philosophic approach to "the daily struggles of men and the passing conflicts of society."

In spite of being so wrapped up in his work, Judge Holmes managed to find time for friendships, old and new, and to take great pleasure in them. Frequently his friends were younger than he was, and often from outside Boston. One of them, Owen Wister, a talented young student at Harvard Law School, became a frequent Saturday or Sunday visitor at the Chestnut Street house. Knowing the Judge's fondness for French novels, Wister might arrive bringing several of them. Holmes warned him that he must be responsible for taking them back as well, for "books borrowed from friends weigh on my soul like lead."

One day Wister received a note from Holmes inviting him to "dine at the vile hour of 2½ at Parker's pothouse tomorrow with the Saturday Club — which is supposed to consist of great swells and is sometimes pleasant and not infrequently dull." Wister was delighted to accept. He was always happy, too, when he could entice the Judge into dining with some of the students in Cambridge and lingering for talk. Later, in writing about Holmes, Wister commented on his liking for using humorous and forceful words, including slang; he remembered Holmes telling a departing guest who he hoped would return, "Don't forget the wittles is served regular."

Harvard's President Eliot was slow to forgive Holmes for preferring the bench to the classroom. It was Yale, not Harvard, which in 1886 conferred on him the honorary degree of Doctor of Laws. Holmes accepted it "proudly as an accolade" and pledged himself to "try to maintain the honor you have bestowed."

Curiously, on that same day, Oliver Wendell Holmes, Sr., received the same honor at Oxford, England. Amelia went over with her father and, with hundreds of his admirers, joined in the thunderous applause as he stood to receive the degree — looking, a reporter said, "like a small gray-headed boy."

Mrs. Holmes did not appreciate the honors which had come to her husband and to her son, for her mind was failing. She was spending the summer quietly at Beverly Farms, thirty miles north of Boston, where a few years before Dr. Holmes had bought a seaside house and where the family now spent each summer. She lingered on for a year or two, then peacefully passed away. Amelia moved in to keep house for her father, but only a year later she was taken ill and died. Once again the aging Dr. Holmes was alone.

For six years the Chestnut Street home had meant the world and all to Wendell and Fanny Holmes. Yet, dearly though they loved it, duty came first and they did not hesitate. The Judge had to go to Springfield to conduct equity court. The moving would be taken care of while he was away, his wife told him. When he returned he should take a cab to 296 Beacon Street. Each knew the feelings of the other, yet there was not a word of complaint. This was clearly the only thing to do — and it was done.

Once more Wendell Holmes became the son of a famous father, living comfortably yet vaguely uncomfortably under his roof. His wife noticed the change at once. An impressive figure on the bench and with his peers, he still seemed almost to squirm under his father's searching eye. He took to stopping in at a club after his day at the Court, or to attending some Boston lady's tea, where he was the social lion. More and more Fanny was left with old Dr. Holmes. She understood. She did not think her husband was very discerning about women; she decided that he was like his father in reveling in their admiration, but if it gave him pleasure, she was glad.

Dr. Holmes loved Fanny and enjoyed having her with him. "Mrs. Judge knows how to make me comfortable and does wonderfully well," he wrote a friend. She was, he said, "a very helpful, hopeful, powerful as well as brilliant woman." He would not go to the theater with "his two young people," but every Sunday morning he attended services at King's Chapel, and he went to Symphony rehearsals and occasionally to a five-o'clock tea. Sometimes the three of them would dine together at the Parker House or at Young's, another favorite eating place, just below Beacon Hill. A hired carriage took them there and back, along Beacon Street past the fine bay-windowed houses and the golden-domed State House.

That first summer after Amelia's death Fanny insisted that her husband go to England, while she and Dr. Holmes spent the warm months at the Holmes place in Beverly Farms. In August the Doctor was eighty. He was pleased at the shower of congratulatory telegrams and notes he received, delighted that friends called and that the village children brought him flowers.

In England, Wendell Holmes threw off the inhibitions of Boston, the Court, and Beacon Street. Here he was known as a distinguished law scholar and judge, a brilliant conversationalist, and a fascinating individual — and he lived up to his reputation. His handsome, youthful appearance, his courtly manners, and his quick mind made him welcome everywhere. He hobnobbed with prominent men of law and of letters and accepted invitations from ladies of high social rank. He especially enjoyed visiting with old friends in and around London, including Pollock — now Sir Frederick — and Henry James at his home in Rye. The summer in England did the Judge worlds of good, as his wife had known it would.

In 1891, a Boston publisher brought out a collection of Judge Holmes's speeches, which he called "chance utterances of faith and doubt." Henry

Justice Holmes about 1890

James spoke of them as beautiful and noble, full of distinction and grace, a "pure and splendid enrichment of English eloquence." Did old Dr. Holmes, turning their pages, ponder over the vast difference between his son's books and his own published work? The aged Doctor was still cheerful and given to puns and lively stories, but each year his small frame shrank a little more. He grew constantly frailer until, in 1894, he faded away completely.

Judge and Mrs. Holmes stayed on in the Beacon Street house. Gradually they replaced some of the Doctor's things with their own, and the house took on at least a little of their personality. The view across the river to Cambridge and the hills beyond remained the same, and Wendell Holmes, like his father before him, never tired of it.

The Judge and his wife also took over the Beverly Farms house and spent almost every summer there. It was a region they both loved. They walked together along the cliffs above the sea or across the wide beaches, or drove along elm-bordered streets through little villages dotted with neat white houses and high-spired churches. Youthful in both body and spirit, though now in his fifties, the Judge bought himself a bicycle and learned to ride it. He wrote Lady Pollock, "I haven't had such a gleam of boyish joy for years as I get from my little runs of five miles or so, all that I have ventured as yet. Even tumbling off was a pleasure — to find that I could do it and not break!"

At last, nine years later than Yale, Harvard recognized its graduate's ability and conferred on Judge Holmes the degree of Doctor of Laws. "I take it as a mark that the President [Eliot] has buried the hatchet and no longer bears me malice for giving up my professorship for a judgeship — which I expressly and in writing reserved the right to do," Holmes wrote Pollock. He was delighted that Pollock was also to receive an LL.D. from Harvard at the same ceremony and was coming to America for it.

Like her husband, Fanny Holmes had always been in remarkably good health. But not long after her father-in-law's death she had a severe siege of rheumatic fever which left her looking and acting totally unlike her former animated self. For months during her slow recovery she seemed tired out and listless, interested in nothing and nobody. For some reason the doctors had thought it would help to have her hair cut short; in that era of long hair this boylike appearance so shamed her that she refused to go out or even to see many of her old friends. Her earlier shyness returned and her tongue, naturally somewhat sharp, grew sharper. More than ever she insisted on her husband's going alone to the theater, to concerts, to dinners, teas, and parties. She did not share his enjoyment of these gatherings and she managed to persuade him that she would be happier at home.

At Beverly Farms the first summer after her illness, Mrs. Holmes insisted on keeping the shades down and the inside of the house in a state of perpetual twilight because the light hurt her eyes. Her husband did not seem to mind — anything Fanny did or wanted to do was all right with him. Besides her birds, she brought in a couple of marmosets and some flying squirrels. Her husband confessed he did not like these, but he tolerated them because he never could deny Fanny anything. Every day they went driving together, which Mrs. Holmes had always enjoyed, and slowly her strength returned.

Wendell Holmes's cousin John Morse undertook to write a life of Dr. Holmes and to collect letters from and to him. Rather to Fanny Holmes's surprise, the Judge made a great effort to help his cousin in every way he could. She was touched by the time and attention he gave to this project, which he evidently thought of as a sort of memorial to his father. What made it even more of a tribute was the fact that the undertaking came at a time when the Judge was especially busy at the Court.

There was labor trouble in Boston — a strike and picketing. The state Supreme Court had handed down an injunction against the picketing, in which Judge Holmes had dissented from his "brethren." It was not illegal for men to patrol, he argued, if they did not use force or physical threats. Some of his conservative friends expressed horror at the "liberal line" the Judge was taking. Holmes knew of their remarks but did not change his mind, though he told a lawyer friend, "I have just handed down an opinion that shuts me off forever from judicial promotion." If the promotion he had in mind was the Chief Justiceship of the state Supreme Court he was wrong, for in three years it was his. Meantime he gave his best to his work, respecting and meeting its every challenge. "No man of any loftiness of soul could be long a Justice of this Court without rising to his full height," he said — and the proof he gave of his own considerable height was ample.

Early in 1897, Judge Holmes spoke at the dedication of the new law school building at Boston University. He called his address "The Path of the Law," and he told his distinguished audience, "Most of the things we do, we do for no better reason than that our fathers have done them. . . . It is revolting to have no better reason for a rule of law than that so it was laid down in the time of Henry IV. It is still more revolting if the grounds upon which it was laid down have vanished since, and the rule simply persists from blind imitation of the past."

His criticism, he said, did not imply disrespect of the law. "I venerate the law and especially our system of law, as one of the vastest products of the human mind. . . . But one may criticize even what one reveres. Law is the business to which my life is devoted, and I should show less than devotion if I did not do what in me lies to improve it."

He told the law students, "If a man goes into law it pays to be a master of it," and he urged them to go to the bottom of the subject and to study the underlying principles of the law. "It is through them that you not only become a great master in your calling, but connect your subject with the universe and catch an echo of the infinite, a glimpse of its unfathomable process, a hint of the universal law."

The next summer Holmes managed to get away again to visit James and other friends in England. Fanny, as usual, spent the time in the Beverly Farms house. She missed her husband, but she was happy with her pet birds and animals, her flowers, and her many visitors. She especially enjoyed the village children, who loved to come to see her and her interesting pets.

As Judge Holmes's mastery of the law grew, so did his reputation and the esteem in which he was held. It really surprised no one when, upon the death of Chief Justice Field in 1899, the Governor appointed Oliver Wendell Holmes (no longer Junior) Chief

Justice of the Supreme Court of Massachusetts. From now on he would be responsible for directing the work of the Court, including assignment to the other six judges of the cases for which they would write up the formal opinions. He assumed these heavier duties without losing his light touch or any of his charm. To Owen Wister he wrote that he was "as busy as a witch in a gale of wind," and to Henry James, "I am firing away at high pressure with breech-loading speed. . . . Generally I feel as keen as I did at twenty and have a deuced sight better time."

Chief Justice Holmes was not in the least impressed with his own importance. He was as impatient of pomposity and pretense as he was of dullness and longwindedness. He picked his friends where he chose, regardless of their social or financial position; he continued to go bicycling about Beverly Farms, and when he wanted to relax by going to a variety show, he went. To an elevator operator who commented on his carrying his own dress-suit case when many judges would not, he said, "I may be poor but I am never proud." Considering his inheritance from his father, neither was he exactly poor.

At a dinner given by the Bar Association of Boston to honor his appointment to the Chief Justiceship, Holmes spoke with feeling about his life and his work. He wondered rather plaintively what he had to show for half a lifetime. He had written up about a thousand cases, he said, "many of them upon trifling or transitory matters," when "one would have liked to study to the bottom and to say his say on every question which the law ever has presented, and then to go on and invent new problems." But, he concluded, "We cannot live our dreams. We are lucky enough if we can give a sample of our best, and if in our hearts we can feel that it has been nobly done."

As Chief Justice of the Massachusetts Supreme Court Oliver Wendell Holmes seemed to have reached the height of his powers and the pinnacle of success. He filled the high place with honor and he felt at home in his work, his home life, with his friends, and in the familiar Boston setting. For three years he performed his duties as Chief Justice with distinction. Then suddenly came another "stroke of lightning." This bolt, even more than the unexpected one which twenty years before had swept him from a Cambridge classroom to a Boston court, was to change his and his wife's life completely.

8

A Great Adventure

PRESIDENT THEODORE ROOSEVELT in August 1902 appointed Oliver Wendell Holmes an Associate Justice of the United States Supreme Court. The appointment had to be confirmed by the Senate when it reconvened later in the year, but no one doubted its approval. Newspapers all over the country commented favorably on the President's choice, though to the dismay of Judge Holmes and his wife nearly all of them said more about his being the son of a famous father than about his qualifications for the high post. Some writers warned that the Massachusetts Judge was brilliant but not very sound, talented but not great. These comments "make one sick," Holmes confided to Pollock, "when he has broken his heart in trying to make every word living and real. . . . If I haven't done my share in the way of putting in new and remodeling old thought for the last twenty years then I delude myself."

At first Wendell Holmes was in some doubt about accepting the appointment. Was he willing to give up his Chief Justiceship of the highest court of the state and his well-established, comfortable life in its capital city? Could he, at sixty-one, adjust himself to life in the nation's capital and to dealing with problems of law on a national rather than a state level? And what about Fanny? Since her illness she had become pretty much of a stay-at-home, caring more for her birds, it almost seemed, than for people.

But it was Fanny Holmes who urged the move to Washington. He had gone as far as he could go in Massachusetts, she told her husband; it was high time for him to become involved in a larger scene and test his talents in a broader field. He need not worry about her; he could depend on her to do whatever the wife of a United States Supreme Court Justice was supposed to do, and to try to do it well.

Fanny Holmes's brave words concealed the terror she felt at the idea of leaving Boston and even more at the thought of the social life she would be expected to lead in Washington. But not for a moment did she let her husband suspect her inner fear or the fact that she was dreadfully self-conscious about her thin face, her skinny body, and her straight gray hair. She even laughed off her lifelong shyness of strangers and declared that she would be delighted to meet some new people. Whatever was best for

Justice Holmes
from a photograph taken about 1902

her husband, Fanny Holmes said over and over to herself, that was the thing — the only thing — to be considered.

Oliver Wendell Holmes was never one to turn his back on a challenge. The opportunity to give greater service to his country appealed to him — far more than the honor of the high post or the slightly better salary it provided.

And so, subject to the almost certain approval of the Senate, the Holmeses began to cut their ties in Boston. The Judge admitted at a Tavern Club dinner that he was feeling this more than he would have expected; that even burning old letters and papers seemed like destroying part of his past. "The roots of sixty years strike deep," he said, "and they cannot be tugged at or cut off without pain." The past twenty years had been the happiest of his life, he told members of the Middlesex Bar Association, and he was finding it "a good deal of a wrench to leave old friends . . . to leave all the associations of a whole life for an unknown new world." Yet it was going to be "a great adventure, and that thought brings with it a mighty joy." It was exciting, too, "to have the chance to do one's share in shaping the laws of the whole country." But when he wrote to Pollock about the move his confidence slipped and he confessed, "Lord, how I tremble at the thought."

The Holmeses were able to rent a furnished house

on Lafayette Square, near the White House. Henry Cabot Lodge, a United States Senator now, had a home not far away, and Henry Adams, who had moved to Washington, lived just around the corner. Immediately after the Senate's approval of his appointment early in December, Wendell Holmes took the night train to Washington. His trusted Irish clerk went with him; Mrs. Holmes would come down with their maids in a few days, after the last tasks of packing and moving out of the Beacon Street house had been attended to. At the Washington station Justice Holmes was met by the elderly Negro who had been the messenger and personal attendant of Justice Gray, Holmes's predecessor on the Court, for twenty years. According to custom, he would now become attached to the new Justice.

Justice Holmes went immediately to call on the President, as etiquette required. Then he walked to the New Willard Hotel, where he would stay until the Lafayette Square house was opened. Meanwhile his Boston clerk went to buy a load of coal, which was temporarily in short supply because of a strike. The clerk returned very much annoyed at having been turned down in several places because none of the coal dealers had ever heard of Oliver Wendell Holmes and claimed that he had no credit in Washington.

Wendell Holmes threw back his head and

laughed. To be unknown and without credit was a completely new experience and he found it highly amusing. After attending to the matter of credit and coal, the Justice was measured for a black silk robe, Supreme Court style. That evening he walked up and down the streets of the capital, as excited as a boy on his first trip away from home.

The following Monday, clad in his new black silk robe, Oliver Wendell Holmes took the two oaths required of an incoming Supreme Court Justice. They were administered by Chief Justice Fuller — the first in the Justices' robing room, across the Capitol corridor from the Supreme Court chamber; the second, a few moments later, in the chamber itself.

Justice Holmes was much moved as, following the marshal, the clerk, the Chief Justice and the eight other black-robed men, he crossed the corridor where Capitol police held back the traffic for the solemn procession, and slowly walked up the center aisle of the Supreme Court chamber. His heart beating rapidly, he took his place behind the last of the nine high black-leather chairs on the raised platform. On this day, as on every day when the Court was in session, the Justices and the spectators — limited to the capacity of the rather small room — remained standing while the clerk of the Court called loudly: "Oyez! Oyez! Oyez! All persons hav-

The former chamber of the United States Supreme Court in the Capitol, Washington, D.C. The Supreme Court sat here when Justice Holmes was a member

ing business with the Supreme Court of the United States draw near and give their attention, for the Court is now sitting. God save the United States and this honorable Court."

As he seated himself, Justice Holmes looked about the gray-walled, marble-pillared, semicircular chamber, feeling anew its aura of dignity, history, and tradition. This room, in the oldest part of the Capitol, had been used by the Senate until it moved into its new chamber just before the Civil War. In the audience the new Justice saw Mrs. Roosevelt and

Mrs. Lodge, and he wished that his wife might have been there too. Presently he stood before Chief Justice Fuller and placed his hand on the Bible — the very one on which John Marshall had been sworn. A wave of deep emotion swept over him as he promised to "administer justice, without respect to persons."

When Fanny Holmes arrived a few days later she took one look at her husband — erect, youthful, exuberant — and knew without doubt that it had been right for them to come to Washington. Weary as she was from the ordeal of closing the Boston house and dreading almost as much the opening of a new one in Washington, she smiled, and the smile seemed to erase the worn lines on her thin face. Here they were, she and Wendell, beginning life all over again at an age when many of their friends were thinking of retiring! Eagerly she turned toward her husband, not wanting to miss a word of his enthusiastic description of his first days in the nation's capital. Truly, this was the start of a great adventure for them both!

9

Beginning All Over Again

LIKE HIS FATHER, Oliver Wendell Holmes enjoyed writing letters. "A letter," he said, "is not a composition but a talk, a breathing out of the casual contents of one's mind." He would stand at the high bookkeeper desk which had been his Grandfather Jackson's and write at top speed in a fine script, preferably on large-sized block paper, because "notepaper cramps me," and "the larger sweep of the arm gives greater freedom to the mind."

Even before the end of his first busy month in Washington he found time to write a few personal letters to congenial friends at a distance. To Sir Frederick Pollock in London he wrote: "Yes — here I am — and more absorbed, interested, and impressed than ever I had dreamed I might be. The work of the past seems a finished book — locked up far away, and a new and solemn volume opens. The variety and novelty to me of the questions, the re-

The Supreme Court of the United States in 1904.
Justice Holmes is at the end of the second row on the left

mote spaces from which they come, the amount of work they require, all help the effect." To Owen Wister he wrote: "Egotism vanishes in the great business to be done. I hope I may do my share nobly, but It not I is the thing one thinks of." And to a Boston friend: "It calls on all one's energies and has so much that is new that in a way it is beginning all over again."

The Supreme Court cases which "absorbed, interested, and impressed" the new Justice were far broader than those he had faced in the Massachu-

setts State Supreme Court. These cases were of
national importance, "involving great interests," he
wrote, "raising questions I have never heard of,
argued by the strongest men the country can show."
Besides deciding matters between the Federal Government and the States, the Court considered problems arising between the individual and his Government, deciding "under what circumstances society
may intervene and when the individual is to be left
unrestricted." Every Supreme Court decision meant
either upholding or reversing the decision of a lower
court, and all decisions were final.

The Justices' guide, the Constitution of the
United States, had been written more than a hundred years before, but written in such general terms
that it could apply to undreamed-of situations in the
far-distant future. Yet different minds — even highly
legal minds — could, and did, interpret those general
terms in different ways. It was Wendell Holmes's
firm belief that the Constitution was built to permit a changing society to "keep step with the march
of the age," and that experimentation within the
law was to be encouraged. Not all of the brethren
shared this view, but however different their ideas,
they treated one another with unfailing courtesy
and respect.

From Monday through Friday the Court session
lasted from noon to four-thirty, with a half-hour

break at two o'clock for a box lunch sent over from the Senate restaurant and served in the robing room. This was something rather new; formerly the Court had sat continuously from noon to four, with the Justices retiring two at a time to "clash their knives and forks" behind the back screen.

Justice Holmes usually walked home from Court, part of the way often in company with one of the other Justices. There was time for a little reading or relaxation before seven, when the Holmeses sat down to a "good but plain" dinner. Frequently there were guests. Mrs. Holmes had the hospitable habit of setting an extra place at the table in case someone unexpectedly dropped in. Some evenings the Holmeses were invited out to dine, and occasionally they would eat at a hotel or restaurant and go on from there to a concert or to the theater, which the Justice thoroughly enjoyed. If something struck him as funny, he would not hesitate to guffaw, sometimes so loudly that it embarrassed his wife. Soon after coming to Washington Justice Holmes was included in a small group of Harvard men invited to the White House every now and then for informal conversation with the President. But the evenings the Holmeses enjoyed most were those spent at home, with Mrs. Holmes reading aloud as her husband relaxed over a game of solitaire, and with him then taking his turn at the reading while his wife knitted.

A month after the Holmeses arrived in Washington President and Mrs. Roosevelt gave a formal dinner party in their honor. This was the sort of thing that Fanny Holmes had dreaded. She dressed conservatively in gray silk, with a high net yoke to cover the thin neck she was ashamed of; she wore long white gloves and at her breast a bunch of violets her husband had brought her. As they entered the White House she concealed her inner timidity by walking straighter than ever. Beside her strode the Justice, handsome in his formal white-tie-and-tails, which accented his thick graying hair, his expressive eyes under the heavy brows, his sweeping mustache, and his splendidly erect tall figure.

The President, coming forward to greet them, claimed Mrs. Holmes as his special companion. His pleasant, informal manner put her at ease and soon she was chatting with him naturally, even wittily, and pleasing him by listening attentively to his stories. Justice Holmes paused in his attentions to the lady beside him to observe the President's pleasure in his wife's company. No cause to worry any more about Fanny, he thought with relief. Why, she was sparkling! If she could hold her own like this with the President, she would soon be charming all official Washington with her quick wit and fine mind — and enjoy doing it, too.

So it happened. Fanny Holmes, like her husband, seemed to take a new lease on life in the exhilarating air of the national capital. She did not relish the formal social life, but she was a perfect hostess and an entertaining conversationalist when at ease with old friends or sympathetic new ones. Delighted, Holmes wrote to a friend of his wife's pleasure in Washington and that she seemed better than she had been for a long time.

That summer President Roosevelt asked Justice Holmes to go to England on a matter of delicate diplomacy having to do with the Alaskan boundary dispute. Holmes, always happy to be in London, was glad to be the President's personal ambassador and accomplished the mission successfully. He was also glad for the chance it gave him to see his English friends and his old companion Henry James, and to visit friends in Ireland.

President Roosevelt was well pleased with his new Supreme Court Justice. He admired his splendid mind, his forceful use of words, his distinguished personality. Best of all in the President's mind was his belief that Holmes was absolutely solid politically. Had he not come out on the side of the laboring man in a Massachusetts court decision, contending that labor had as much right to combine as did capital? The new Justice would be a great help in the all-out fight he, the President, was waging against big business and the trusts. When a trust got too big, he intended to "bust" it, if not by legislative, then by judicial, means.

What Theodore Roosevelt did not realize was that the former Massachusetts Chief Justice had never once made a decision in order to favor any class above any other. What he had always tried to do was to apply the law with absolute fairness to all. Even Senator Lodge, who had known Holmes all his life and whom Roosevelt had consulted before making the appointment, did not fully appreciate this impartial attitude.

President Roosevelt counted on Justice Holmes's support when the Northern Securities case, involving a big business merger, came up to the Supreme Court. The majority of the Court satisfied Roosevelt by declaring the merger illegal, but not by the overwhelming vote he had expected. And to his amazement and wrath, Justice Holmes did not vote with the majority. Completely unswayed by the well-known feelings of the President and by the opinions of his brethren, this newest Justice dared to dissent. His argument was that bigness in itself was no crime, and that in a growing society combinations were to be expected. The President, who could not forgive anyone for standing in the way of what he wanted done, was so angry with Holmes that for a time he considered forbidding him to set foot in the White House. Roosevelt was persuaded not to do this, but relations between the two men became very strained, in spite of Holmes's seeming indifference to the President's hostility.

Their first fall in Washington the Holmeses bought and moved into a four-story brick house at 1720 I Street. It was exactly two miles from the Capitol, which the Justice considered just a brisk walk. In appearance the new house was not too different from the Beacon Street one, but this home was their own. "A pleasant place in a modest way," the Justice described it to Lewis Einstein, a literary and diplomatic friend he had made since coming to Washington. "The sun streams in at the back, and I feel that I am settled for good in a place which is mine. The Boston house never ceased to be my father's. . . . I am very happy here."

There were fireplaces over which Wendell Holmes put some of his family treasures, and a chandelier from which Fanny Holmes dangled a miniature skeleton with springy arms and legs that she delighted to set to jiggling when she passed by. Many books and pictures, rugs, attractive lamps, and comfortable chairs made the place homelike. The Justice set up his study on the second floor at the front; his books lined its walls and those of the small room behind it. It took him one very long day to arrange them on the ceiling-to-floor shelves, but: "Oh, the heavenly joy," he wrote Einstein, "to see order where there was confusion . . . to see what one has . . . and to find things one didn't even know one owned." Some of his books were old — "not valuable enough to be a worry but taking one back. I like to think that this or that volume was standing in a bookcase before America was discovered."

There were no private offices for the Supreme Court Justices; they must do their work at home. Every morning Justice Holmes spent some time at his broad old-fashioned desk before setting out precisely at eleven-thirty to walk to the Capitol for the noon opening of the Court. He wrote his opinions in longhand and looked up most of his legal references in the law books on his own shelves.

The Government provided each Justice with the services of a messenger — a sort of body servant — and of a secretary. At first Justice Holmes did not think he needed a secretary; then he was persuaded to try one for a year. Most of the Justices had a stenographer-typist, but Holmes decided he would prefer to have a law clerk fresh from law school. He asked Professor Gray, his good friend and successor at Harvard Law School, to select from among the honor students of the graduating class a young man interested in spending a year in Washington. The year should not be without value to the young man, thought Holmes, and for him it would a refreshing way to keep up with new ideas.

These secretaries — a different one each year — came to be known as "Holmes's Annuals." The secretary's duties, Holmes told each one as he arrived (always late in the week preceding the fall opening of the Court) were to handle the mail, summarize the certiorari (the applications for Supreme Court hearings which the Justices must decide on), keep the docket of cases up to date, look up legal references, balance the Justice's checkbook ("accounts drive me mad"), and listen to his "tall talk." He impressed on the young men the need to keep healthy, to work hard, and to keep an open mind. "If you're a credit to me and I'm a credit to you," he told them, "then we'll both have something to brag about."

To every one of the "Annuals," the year with Justice Holmes was indeed one to remember and "to brag about." He and his wife treated the young men like the sons they did not have. They intended, the Justice said, to have "all the pleasures of parenthood without any of the responsibilities." Mrs. Holmes mothered them; her husband talked to them as to intellectual equals.

One important responsibility of the secretary, as

he sat at his desk in the small room adjoining the Justice's study, was to enter the number and essential data on each case assigned to Justice Holmes in the docket book. This was a locked red-leather book with steel back. At the bottom of each page was a space for noting the way each Justice voted and the comments he made on the case at the Saturday conference.

These private Saturday conferences — "jaws," Justice Holmes irreverently called them — were held in a small room on the floor beneath the Court chamber. A wide range of views was expressed there — informally and often brilliantly, but always with due regard for each man's opinion. After the Justices summed up their reactions to the cases they had heard argued, the Chief Justice called for votes, beginning with the newest Justice and ending with himself. Then he assigned to various Justices the writing of the formal opinions.

Each Monday morning Justice Holmes would begin work on writing up the opinions of the cases assigned to him. His secretary might help him look up references, but the amount of law knowledge that the Justice carried in his head was amazing. So was his ability to spot quickly the reference he wanted in the Year Books — the official records of past cases. When the opinion was written, often with many changes and strikeouts and additions, it was sent to the Government printer to be set into type. This was done in strictest secrecy, with exactly nine proofs pulled. On receiving his copy each Justice would make his criticisms or suggestions on its wide margins, then return the proof to the original writer. Wherever he could reasonably do so, the writer would incorporate the suggested changes into the opinion, to make it acceptable to all — a unanimous opinion. Preparing a readable final revision from the much altered and interlined proof was sometimes (as Dean Acheson, once Justice Louis Brandeis's secretary, tells in his *Morning and Noon*) a scissors-and-paste job for the secretary, resulting in a set of pages requiring an expert typesetter to decipher.

Justice Holmes considered himself "pretty accommodating" in cutting out ideas he would have liked to see included in an opinion and in yielding his views to those of the other brethren. He would often rework an opinion to soften it "so that it can be swallowed." But if the disagreements were too great to be ironed out or softened, there would be, in addition to the majority opinion, one or more dissenting opinions, which the dissatisfied Justice or Justices would write to express their own particular views.

During the Court session Justice Holmes jotted down important points in the lawyers' arguments.

He came to his decision with sureness and with speed, and he wrote up his opinions in the same way. His style was noted for its strength and clearness — a reflection of the strength and clearness of his thinking. In addition, his sentences had a delightful charm and grace — and often wit. His opinions had logic and insight, power and vitality — and they were short; the Justice hated loose, wordy, pretentious prose. Francis Biddle, one of the "Annuals," commented that after the Justice went to Washington his style became "terser, more inevitable. . . . His words were feathered arrows that carried to the heart of the target, from a mind that searched and saw."

Justice Holmes believed that style was largely "sound, a matter of ear," and he liked to express his thoughts "with a singing variety." He was very conscious of the beauty of style in others' writings, and susceptible to it. After reading Homer's *Odyssey* he commented, "Like Dante, though to a lesser degree, the song of the words added to the sense seems sometimes to open a road to paradise." Dante was his greatest literary passion. He once wrote Wister that he had been so thrilled with "the intensity of Dante's spiritual rapture" that he "had to rush out of doors and walk it off."

Justice Holmes's eye for beauty was not confined to words. All his life he liked to take a second look at a pretty woman, and he enjoyed few things more than talking to women with charm (which he thought rarer than intellect) "with just a touch of gallantry — it shakes one out of the law." He also responded to the beauties of nature, especially those that came in the spring. Each year he liked to spot the first crocuses on the White House lawn and to revel with his wife in the cherry blossoms — "endless billows of pink and white" — reflected in the Potomac Basin.

The year after the Northern Securities dissent which so angered President Theodore Roosevelt, Justice Holmes dissented in another important case. This one involved the right of a state to pass laws with a view to improving social conditions. When New York State passed a law that prohibited bakery employees from working more than ten hours a day, a baker named Lochner claimed that it violated his rights as an employer. Most of the Justices of the United States Supreme Court, where the case was appealed, agreed with him, and the majority opinion called the law "a meddlesome interference" of the state into individual rights.

Justice Holmes saw it otherwise. In his dissenting opinion he argued that laws must keep up with a fast-changing society and that state legislators were in a better position to know local needs than were the members of the Supreme Court; they should be left free to legislate social experiments unless the United States Constitution expressly forbade it. Although this was a minority opinion, it was important in indicating legal and social trends, as dissents frequently were. Later on it became the view held by the majority of the Supreme Court and overruled their first opinion — a reversal which clearly showed the Justice to be a man ahead of his time, as did many other of Holmes's dissents.

The life of a Supreme Court Justice was not an easy one, either physically or mentally, but Mr. Justice Holmes, with his active mind and body, thoroughly enjoyed it. He rarely missed a session and gladly took on more than his share of cases to write up. If the work was too heavy to finish in the mornings before going to Court he would put in a few hours at his desk after his return. While he worked his secretary might have tea with Mrs. Holmes in her little sitting room behind the study annex where he sat. The Justice rarely joined them, saying he did not want to spoil his dinner. Very rarely he went back to his study in the evening; usually evenings and Sundays were devoted to relaxation — except for the customary Sunday call on the Chief Justice.

In 1910, President Taft had appointed Associate Justice Edward White Chief Justice of the Supreme Court. Justice White was a Southerner who had been on the Court for many years and who in his youth had served in the Confederate Army. Each day, as the judicial procession formed to enter the Supreme Court chamber, Justice Holmes roguishly gave a precise military salute to his former enemy, now his good friend. And each year, on the anniversary of one of the battles in which Holmes was wounded, Justice White would present him with a red rose, which he proudly pinned onto his black silk robe.

Important people with interesting minds were sure of a welcome in the hospitable Holmes house. They were also sure of what was commonly said to be the best conversation in Washington. It might be of the "unimproving" variety, guaranteed to relax or, more likely, a sparkling exchange of brilliant thought. If the Justice happened to meet a man who seemed to him exceptionally well informed on some subject he was interested in, or with a quality of mind which appealed to him, he did not hesitate to invite him to the I Street home for a good "chin" or "jaw." Friends were welcome, Mrs. Holmes let it be known, any time up to two o'clock in the morning.

Monday was an important day for Mrs. Holmes. It was the "At Home" day of the Justices and their wives, their day to be called on. On Monday afternoon every Justice hurried away promptly after Court to be at home when his wife served tea to

visiting celebrities, writers, young lawyers, men connected with the Government — and their wives and
guests. At the Holmeses', the current secretary presented the newcomers, and a couple of younger
ladies assisted Mrs. Holmes at the tea table. The
Justice's admirers would make a ring about him,
prepared to laugh at his ready wit and gather up
some clever saying to repeat at their next call. Mrs.
Holmes was an impeccable hostess, very capable of
holding her own in these traditional social affairs.
Once, however, Dean Acheson relates, "Without a
word of warning and at a moment of perfect peace
General Pershing and his staff appeared in over-
powering military array and brilliance, leaving even
indomitable Mrs. Holmes limp."

Seventeen-twenty I Street was a lively, light-
hearted household. Every holiday and anniversary
was celebrated in some original way, and there were
many funny little personal jokes and tricks. On the
first day of April Mrs. Holmes always tried to fool
her husband with trick bugs, matches, blots, or some
such silly trifle. Beginning a personal letter one day
by setting down the date and noticing that it was
April 1, the Justice stopped long enough to "go
downstairs to practice a little surprise on my wife by
way of an April Fool." What it was, he did not say,
but when he continued his letter he reported, "It

was fairly successful — enough so as to make her try to box my ears."

Usually in the late winter or early spring there was a two- or three-week recess of the Court to allow the Justices to catch up in the preparation of the opinions they had to write. Justice Holmes was often annoyed at the length of time it took some of the men to do this. "Whether my work is good or bad," he wrote his friend Einstein, "at least it is rapid, which I regard as an important element in decisions. I think that to let cases hang for months after they have been argued is discreditable." With his fast-working mind — and pen — he could pride himself on keeping his work up to date, even when it meant such preparation as "reading through over two thousand pages of longwinded cases on the antitrust law." He might complain about being "a slave of the lamp and the pen," but he was truly happiest when pitting his mind against a tough legal problem. He wrote a brilliant young English friend, Harold Laski, of concentrating on "a case of frightful impact with fierce intensity. I fear that my brethren or some of them will think I should have taken a month. But I always say that it is impact not dead pull that drives a pile and I think I have seen and stated the points."

On days when the Court was not in session Justice and Mrs. Holmes liked to drive around the capital city. Washingtonians grew accustomed to the sight of the handsome Justice and his lady being driven by their decorous coachman Charley in a neat little carriage behind a fast-enough but not too high-stepping horse. They liked to ride along the Potomac or through Rock Creek Park, stopping at favorite beauty spots. And they frequently visited the zoo to see the newly added animals and to check up on their favorites.

To the surprise of many of their friends, and not a little to their own, Justice and Mrs. Holmes came to feel almost as much at home in Washington as in their native Boston. They grew to love the city and to sink their roots into it deeply. Life in the national capital was for them a rich and satisfying experience — truly a "beginning all over again."

10

North Shore Summers

In Late May or early June the Supreme Court adjourned for the summer. The push to complete all opinions meant strenuous days for the Justices, even for quick-minded, rapid-writing Justice Holmes. After the final Saturday conference the nine learned men would celebrate the end of the term with supper together, then part for the summer months.

Justice Holmes admitted that when the work of the Court stopped he felt at first as if the bottom had dropped out of life "with the machinery still going inside and nothing for it to work upon. I sadly fear that I am industrious." Yet, like his wife, he welcomed the summer months when they would escape from Washington's heat and relax in their cool and comfortable Beverly Farms home.

The train ride north was likely to be hot and tiring, and the Holmeses usually stopped over in Boston for a day or two while the servants went on to open up the summer place. Their maid Annie knew all the ropes, for she had been going to Beverly Farms almost every year since Dr. Holmes bought the house. In the city Justice and Mrs. Holmes would see a few friends and perhaps go to a movie, and the Justice would have his hair cut by his favorite barber. But they were always impatient to put the last thirty miles of their journey behind them and to sniff the "living air" and salt breezes of the North Shore.

The unpretentious brown wooden house was set against rocks high above the road and approached by a gravel drive bordered with flowers. The flowers meant almost as much to Fanny Holmes as did her birds. She was proud of her roses, and she tended them and her petunias, marigolds, geraniums, delphiniums, and cannas with loving care. But for the first few days after their arrival both she and her husband did little more than abandon themselves to "the joy of the air, the trees, the ocean." After a hard year's work the Justice said he felt entitled to "keep my mind empty, bike in a pottering way of an afternoon, play solitaire and read little, not bothering about improving my mind."

The Holmeses knew most of the oldtimers in the little village and were known and liked by them. Each day the Justice walked to the post office, stopping to chat with the watchman at the railroad crossing, "who has a touch of poetry in his make-up." They talked about the watchman's children and about his dog; they exchanged views on the state of the world; and they commented on the changes that came year by year to the village, laughing together about the name of old Screeching Beach being changed to Singing Beach and that of the Misery Islands to the Mystery Islands.

In the afternoons the Holmeses liked to walk along the shore or drive beside the rugged rocks and curving stretches of seaswept sands. "Among the foundations of my soul are granite rocks and barberry bushes," the Justice said. Usually they would "toddle round behind a single horse, jawing with the driver," but increasingly with the years, and especially when they had a more distant objective in mind or when showing the beauties of the region to a guest, they would hire an "odious automobile." The automobile, the Justice commented, "somewhat takes the wonder out of things by bringing them so near. In the days of horses the Cape [Ann] would be full of remote mysteries that I might hope to pry into one by one. Now we can go round half the show in two hours. But the charm to me is too great for familiarity to blunt it. It goes back to my first impressions as a child." Both of them loved this whole North Shore region. "I don't know Paradise by name," Justice Holmes said, "but I must have seen most of it."

Walking, driving, entertaining, resting, reading, writing — the summers at Beverly Farms were both pleasurable and relaxing. But after "the vastly pleasant idleness" of the first few weeks the Justice began the summer's duty of going over his share of the certiorari to be examined — those applications to bring to the Supreme Court cases where, as the Justice explained to a friend, "it is not a matter of right but depends on our discretion."

To help examine the sacks of "certs" which arrived at Beverly Farms, the secretary of the year spent part of the vacation period with the Holmeses. The relationship was as happy here as in Washington. Affectionately calling the young man "Sonny," "Young Feller," "Lad," "Boy," or even "Young Idiot," the Justice would encourage him to express his views and would listen attentively to his reasoning. When one of them confessed to not understanding a sentence Justice Holmes had written, the Justice sighed and picked up his pen to rewrite it. "If you don't understand it," he said, "there may be some other darn fool who won't." But another time, when the secretary declared that not one man in a thousand would understand a certain paragraph, Justice Holmes let it stand, saying briefly, "I write for that man."

At Beverly Farms, as in Washington, everything was done in longhand. The Justice wanted no clattering typewriter around. He enjoyed the feel of a pen in his hand, both when writing on legal matters and, even more, when visiting on paper with friends. He could write anywhere — standing up at the high desk in his Washington study, on the bench before him at the Court, at his flat-topped desk, on a table, or on his lap. Nor was he easily disturbed by distractions, predictable or unpredictable.

The Beverly Farms house was always filled with Fanny's pets, and one summer the Justice wrote to his friend Einstein, "The blot above was caused by the tyrant of the house, a white kitten, jumping from a chair to my lap and thence to the table and walking across my paper. He is fond of doing it, and when I am reading to my wife of an evening he hops up and sits on my book." The Justice had almost as soft a heart for animals as did his wife. One summer both were saddened when, on the advice of a veterinarian, they had a pet cat, "the noblest cat in the world," put to sleep and afterward decided that it might not have been necessary.

Reading was the Holmeses' delight in summer even more than during the winter months, and at Beverly Farms reading aloud was their usual evening pastime, "so far as her eyes and my voice let us," said the Justice. As in Washington he enjoyed playing a game of solitaire while his wife read aloud, though he confessed it was a bit "unfavorable to listening acutely." They never lacked for interesting reading matter and sampled a great variety, finding themselves bored by some of the modern novelists "who take themselves too seriously." The Beverly Farms librarian would save books for them when she thought they were about due to arrive, always including a pile of mysteries for the Justice. He would skip through dozens of detective stories and French novels in a summer. Once he confessed rather guiltily to reading four detective stories in a row while his secretary was away for a brief time. But he always had heavier reading in hand too. A steady diet of light reading, he said, made him feel as if he had been eating too many chocolates. "I feel I am not doing what I should," he wrote a friend, "unless I have some more serious and more or less difficult work on hand for reading in the summertime. But it is delightful when one's conscience is put to rest and, as yesterday, one can get upon a lounge with half a dozen unimproving books and dip and doze."

At Beverly Farms the Holmeses had even more visitors than in Washington. Their old Boston friends came out for luncheon or to pay an afternoon call; Cambridge friends came too, and some from much farther away. There were guests from distant parts of the country and from England and

Ireland. Many of those who came to see the Holmeses were considerably younger than they, for age differences never mattered in the least to either of them. When the Justice said, "It is a great privilege to be allowed to associate with the (relatively) young on equal terms," he was expressing his wife's feeling as well as his own.

Some years Mrs. Holmes spent the first part of the summer alone at Beverly Farms while her husband vacationed in England. His many friends there made much of him and filled his days and evenings with enjoyable activities. "I always feel twice the man I was after I visited London," he said. Sometimes he would get in a quick trip to Paris, and occasionally to Ireland, where there was a Roman Catholic priest whose friendship he especially valued. He thoroughly enjoyed the relaxation of the ocean voyage, too, breathing in the salt air, reading and resting and having interesting conversations with fellow travelers. But he always returned to Beverly Farms in time to spend the tail end of the summer with his wife there and to attend to the "certs" which had accumulated.

In the late summer of 1907 he wrote to a friend from Ireland, "I have been paying a visit of affection to England, seeing old friends, not bothering at making new ones." He missed his wife and doubted that he would make the trip again unless he could persuade her to go with him. But he knew that the idea of a voyage across the Atlantic terrified her and that she much preferred Beverly Farms to London.

Two years later the Justice did return to England — alone — to receive at Oxford the degree of Honorary Doctor of Common Law. This time he stayed only three weeks, most of the time in and around London, before returning, refreshed and ready for the task of examining the waiting stacks of certiorari.

In 1912 the Justice made the much shorter journey across Massachusetts to receive an honorary degree and make a speech at Williams College in Williamstown. "A beautiful place," he called it. He was always happy to get back to the Berkshires, which held happy memories of his boyhood vacations and of his recruiting expeditions during Civil War days, and where he still had many friends.

It pleased the Justice when the Massachusetts Bar Association commissioned a portrait painter to paint his likeness for the Supreme Judicial Court of Massachusetts. Painter Wilton Lockwood set up his easel in a barn across the road from the Holmes house and each morning at ten the Justice sauntered over to pose for him — standing. The result was a touch of painful lumbago, but the portrait was worth it. "A great success," Justice Holmes commented happily, declaring that the painter had "got some insides as well as outsides." He and Mrs. Holmes attended the presentation dinner where there were many important persons who, the Justice said, "really did what they could to make me think myself a great man."

Every year the time to close up the old brown house and return to Washington came all too soon. As the Justice wrote to his friend Pollock one September, "The vacation has gone by on wings, and I hardly have had enough to show for it, even enough idleness."

11

Justice Brandeis—and
the First Amendment

By law, a Supreme Court Justice can retire on full pay for the rest of his life after his seventieth year. This arrangement did not interest Justice Holmes in the least. He might be seventy, incredible though it seemed to him and to others, but he was still vigorous in mind and body. He told inquiring reporters that he did not intend to quit work "till work ceased to be fun," and he wrote Pollock to tell his wife that "the old man went round the last post to the home stretch going strong."

The Justice was careful to keep himself in good physical trim. He still walked the two miles to and from his home and the Capitol, though he sometimes accepted a ride part way home from the Chief Justice or one of the brethren. Usually a friend or his secretary walked with him, and they would stop to look at the plants in the botanical gardens at the foot of Capitol Hill or detour a bit to stroll through the Smithsonian or the White House grounds.

Reporters were a little annoyed that Justice Holmes would not give interviews and that he did not wish to be "written up" in the papers. Those covering the Supreme Court sessions would sometimes mention his habit of making rapid notes as the lawyers presented their arguments and then sitting back with closed eyes as if he had already summed up the case in his mind and come to a decision. They noticed that occasionally he would suddenly sit bolt upright, extend a long forefinger, and shoot at a young lawyer a difficult, unexpected question. And they were impressed to come across Justice Holmes in the Court library, which was beneath the Court chamber, poring over Year Books of law cases as absorbed as if he were reading a current novel.

Neither did the Justice often write articles or make speeches. "So long as I am capable of my best," he said, "I want to put it into my work." So it was not surprising that even after ten years on the Court his name was not familiar to Americans in general, though it was well known in the legal world both in the United States and in Great Britain. When the name of Oliver Wendell Holmes was mentioned most Americans would still think of the Justice's father, author of "Old Ironsides," "The Deacon's One-Hoss Shay," and other favorites of theirs.

Oliver Wendell Holmes, Sr., had reveled in the publicity his writing brought him. His son, loving his work as a jurist, preferred to pour his time and talent into it. On the rare occasions when he turned from it to make a speech, it was an event. Now, as the chief speaker at the 1911 celebration of the fiftieth anniversary of his graduation from Harvard, he was concerned about what he should say.

Turning his mind to the past, the Justice thought of all that had happened to him in the half century since he had received his college diploma. His three years' war experiences were so vivid to him that even after nearly fifty years he still could not bear to read about the Civil War. Felix Frankfurter, long-time professor at Harvard Law School, later Supreme Court Justice, and close friend of the Justice for many years, called that conflict the most important single influence in Justice Holmes's life. It was constantly evident in his soldierly bearing, in his many military turns of speech, in his strong sense of duty, and in his passionate love of country.

After the war, the Justice remembered the long years of legal study and of establishing himself as a law scholar, his teaching at Harvard, and then his twenty years on the bench in Boston and now ten more on the nation's highest court. All in all, he decided, it was the early years which had influenced him most — his youth in and around Boston and his experiences at college and in the war.

Still in search of ideas for the anniversary address,

the Justice reread a few of his old speeches. The summer before he and Fanny moved to Washington he had spoken at the unveiling of some memorial stones in the historic town of Ipswich, a few miles north of Beverly Farms. He read aloud: "We all, the most unbelieving of us, walk by faith. We do our work and live our lives not merely to vent and realize our inner force, but with a blind and trembling hope that somehow the world will be a little better for our striving." He pondered over that and decided that it expressed the philosophy of most of that notable class of 1861, of whom nearly two thirds had, like him, gone into battle for their country.

And so Justice Holmes wrote his speech. In it he said: "Life is painting a picture, not doing a sum. . . . I learned in the regiment and in the class the conclusion, at least, of what I think the best service that we can do for our country and for ourselves: To see so far as one may, and to feel, the great forces that are behind every detail . . . to hammer out as compact and solid a piece of work as one can, to try to make it first rate, and to leave it unadvertised."

Early in 1913, Justice Holmes was persuaded to make another speech, this one before the Harvard Law School Association of New York. Here he urged that judges "learn to transcend our own convictions and to leave room for much that we hold dear to be done away with short of revolution by the orderly change of law." More personally, he expressed his "faith in a universe not measured by our fears, a universe that has thought and more than thought inside of it."

That summer Justice Holmes went again to England. It was his last visit there, for the dark days of World War I were upon the world. The coming of war saddened him. "I loathe war," he wrote Pollock after his return. "But I think that man at present is predatory, and . . . between two groups that want to make inconsistent kinds of worlds I see no remedy except war."

To his friend and faithful correspondent Lewis Einstein, overseas in diplomatic service, he wrote that the war, which he supposed was inevitable, filled him with sorrow, "apart from its effect upon us and from my personal sympathy with England. . . . Though I don't read the papers, the war makes it hard for me not to be unhappy, anxious, sad to be out of it." He recalled how, as a young soldier, he had cried because he was hospitalized and unable to lead his men at the battle of Fredericksburg, then he philosophized, "I take advantage of my age and try to remain serene, I won't say detached, in the midst of war." But, he added, "My serenity, such as it is, is based on the conviction that worry is a futile waste of energy." Meantime he put all the money he could spare into United States bonds.

The young men in World War I compared favorably with the soldiers of his youth, the Justice thought. "I feel better about my country when I see what tidy looking chaps they are in khaki," he said, and added that this war was being conducted in a more businesslike and intelligent way than the Civil War. In the dark days of 1918, he wrote Einstein that he was "not without hope. . . . The war covers the whole sky now, but you will live until it becomes a distant memory. Beauty is not destroyed from the face of the earth, and nature has a longer wind than man."

Louis Brandeis, a good friend whom the Justice had known many years before at Harvard Law School, was appointed to the Supreme Court during the war years. The Senate took a long time to confirm his appointment, fearful that he was too interested in social reform to be as objective as a member of the nation's highest court should be. President Wilson called him a "friend of justice and of men," and no one denied that he was devoted to the welfare of his country, as well as being a master of figures and facts. Brandeis shared Justice Holmes's belief that the Constitution was intended to promote, not hinder, progress, and that experimental legislation should be encouraged in both nation and state.

After Louis Brandeis came to Washington he and

Justice Holmes became close friends. Their backgrounds were very different, yet their way of looking at things was much the same, and they shared the same wholehearted devotion to the Constitution and to their country. Holmes had a deep respect for Brandeis's mind and for his legal ability. Able lawyers, Holmes declared, could be divided into three classes — kitchen knives, razors, and stings. Louis Brandeis, he said, was a sting.

One of the first of many cases in which Justices Holmes and Brandeis dissented from the majority decision had to do with child labor. Congress, trying to stop the employment of children in factories, had passed a law which made it illegal for goods made by children to be shipped across state borders. Five of the Supreme Court Justices said that this law was unconstitutional because it interfered with matters which should be left to the states. The other four, including Holmes and Brandeis, believed that the law did not "meddle with anything belonging to the States" but was concerned with a matter of national welfare which it was the business of Congress to look after. Brandeis's motive in dissenting was his great desire to improve the living and working conditions of all people; Holmes's motive was his belief that the Constitution warranted legislative effort to promote the national good.

During World War I, Justice Holmes was greatly

concerned about the curbs Congress placed on the freedom of speech. He valued the First Amendment, with its guarantee of free speech and press, above every other principle in the Constitution. But he did not underestimate the problem of the war, and he agreed that nothing must be allowed to interfere with the war effort, not even the protection of free speech.

The Espionage Act, passed by Congress in 1917, "penalized any attempt to cause disloyalty in the Army or Navy or to obstruct recruiting." Three cases — the Schenck, Frowerk, and Debs cases — where the defendants had been found guilty under this Act, came before the Supreme Court. All of them pleaded that the guarantee of free speech provided by the First Amendment had been violated. Each time the Justices denied the plea and voted unanimously to uphold the conviction. And each time the Chief Justice assigned to Justice Holmes the writing and delivery of the opinion, knowing that he would be the most convincing spokesman for the Court, both because of his masterful use of words and because of his well-known belief in freedom of speech.

Perhaps it was because he hated to write these opinions, as he later confessed, that he wrote them so effectively that they became classics of clear, forceful logic. In the Schenck case he explained that every act depended on the circumstances in which it was done. "The most stringent protection of free speech would not protect a man in falsely shouting fire in a theater and causing a panic. . . . The question in every case is whether the words are used in such circumstances and are of such a nature as to create a clear and present danger. . . . When a nation is at war many things that might be said in time of peace are such a hindrance to its effort that their utterance will not be endured . . ."

Justice Holmes's "clear and present danger" phrase became a test for judging other freedom-of-speech cases. Justice Brandeis called it a "rule of reason," for it provided that fine point of balance between the right of free expression and the necessary protection of a nation at war.

Some of the radical friends of the convicted men in the Debs case were so angry at Justice Holmes's opinions that they threatened to blow him up. A bomb mailed to him was stopped at the post office, and for a while, as a protection but against the Justice's wishes, a policeman was stationed outside his door. It was the usually imperturbable Mrs. Holmes who was most upset by this threat to her husband.

Once the war was won and the question of immediate danger to the country had subsided, Justice Holmes saw the matter of free speech differently. He felt that now the First Amendment should come into its own again, and that Congress no longer had any constitutional right to limit the free expression of opinion.

In the Abrams case, a few ardent Russians were convicted and sentenced to twenty years in jail for printing some leaflets which protested the United States Government's sending American troops into Russia after the 1917 revolution there. The majority of the Supreme Court upheld this conviction, but neither Justice Holmes nor Justice Brandeis agreed with them. Three of the Justices, writes Dean Acheson, who was Justice Brandeis's secretary at the time, called on Justice Holmes and took Mrs. Holmes into his study with them. They urged him not to dissent in the Abrams case but to stick with the other Justices and make the opinion a unanimous one. It was a friendly call and the arguments were presented quietly and not pressed. Justice Holmes also was friendly, even affectionate toward his callers as he told them regretfully that he could not change his mind. Presumably this story was told by his secretary, who was seated unseen but within hearing in the adjoining room.

Justice Holmes's dissent in the Abrams case made history. It was so eloquent a plea for the freedom of expression that, said Professor Samuel J. Konefsky, "It is likely to endure as long as human freedom itself remains a faith which men live by." In it, Justice Holmes said that in his opinion the Government had not been threatened by this group of Russians, and that they had had a perfect right to express themselves and their views in the way they did. The best test of truth, said the Justice, was to give all ideas — especially "opinions that we loathe" — a chance to be heard and judged. In time, people would sort out the true from the false, and reason would prevail over error.

Among Justice Holmes's many overseas friends Frederick Pollock and Lewis Einstein were the ones with whom he corresponded most often. In 1916, at seventy-five, Holmes added to the list of regulars Harold Laski, a young Englishman whom Felix Frankfurter brought up to Beverly Farms from Harvard, where Laski was a junior instructor. As Frankfurter anticipated, the two men found each other stimulating, charming, and congenial. In a letter to Pollock, Holmes described Harold Laski as "the very most learned man I ever saw of any age . . . now in his twenties and an extraordinarily agreeable chap."

The half-century difference in age seemed not to matter at all; their minds obviously operated on the same wave length. For the four years Laski remained in Cambridge he wrote the Justice almost every week and often sent him books and articles he thought would be of special interest. Unless the pressure of work was too great, Holmes would answer immediately, usually discussing and adding to the subjects Laski had mentioned in his letter. As with Einstein and Pollock, sometimes these letters would be scribbled in Court — once "pending a reargument in which I have made up my mind." The lawyers, Holmes commented dryly, were no doubt crediting him with taking more than his usual number of notes on their arguments.

From their first friendly tone the letters to Laski took on an affectionate note, with the Justice calling his young correspondent "My dear lad" and even "My son." Along with Felix Frankfurter, Harold Laski had, the Justice admitted, "walked deep into my heart." Occasionally Laski visited the Holmeses in Washington or at Beverly Farms. When he left Cambridge for London the Justice wrote him, "I shall miss you sorely," and begged him to continue to write, for there were "no words to say how stimulating" his letters were. Laski did go on writing; the correspondence continued throughout Justice Holmes's life.

All through his seventies the Justice remained extraordinarily vigorous. Once in a while he had a touch of lumbago, which never was serious enough to keep him from Court, though once he had to be helped to his feet when the Justices rose. In his middle seventies he complained of being "shut up for a week with the grippe; the first time so far as I remember that I have ever missed being present in Court." But he began to give up his long walks and some of his outside activities, finding that his work took just about all the energy he had. "While the term is on," he wrote, "I hardly have time to do more than hear arguments, write decisions, take my victuals and breathe."

Yet he did occasionally find time to go to the Library of Congress for informative talks about engravings and etchings with the curator of prints, and to visit an engraving shop to "stretch his purse" for an etching or two. On one rainy New Year's Day he stayed home instead of making the customary calls and pored over a new issue of the *Print Collectors' Quarterly*. This art, which had delighted him in his boyhood, might be neglected for years at a time but it never lost its appeal for him and whenever he found time he returned to it.

Justice Holmes was now becoming much better known. On his seventy-fifth birthday the *Harvard Law Review* and the *Illinois Law Review* dedicated their monthly issues to him. Their tributes, the Justice confessed, made him feel "pretty happy. . . . It gives one a kind of support in the battle of the present to believe that the past has been a success." He excused his pleasure on the grounds that "when a man is going on eighty he has a right to be pleased with a bit of praise now and then. I dare say that we all should be none the worse if we got more of it." Age, he said, was bringing to him the self-respect he had tried for unsuccessfully all his life.

On that seventy-fifth birthday Mrs. Holmes, who never forgot a holiday or an anniversary, "had a few quiet people in to dine," the Justice wrote Einstein. "After they left, as a complete surprise to me, my wife had arranged to have all the young people (relatively young) who come and play with us on Monday afternoons gather here. The first I knew was hearing the house filled with the song of birds, as she had provided them all with bird calls, and there was a little supper and a pleasing bowl of punch. We giggled and made giggle, as Cowper says, till after midnight, and I was really touched and pleased."

Young people's affection for the Justice was explained by Harold Laski this way: "Partly, this is because he takes endless pains to understand them; partly because he is always so anxious to give them of his best." Dean Acheson testified that to a young man association with the Justice was "intoxicating," and he commented, "He gave the young a sense of great community of interest by his joy, eagerness, and delight in the beauty of life." The Justice himself said merely, "We encourage each other," and he claimed that the knowledge of the young overwhelmed him and kept him modest.

It was always Fanny Holmes who contributed the

most to the Justice's happiness and youthfulness. She was as high-spirited and fun-loving as he, continually thinking of clever, amusing things to do and say, and ways to add to his comfort and pleasure. She delighted in their many friends and their expeditions in and around the city and their frequent visits to the zoo. Her husband seemed to enjoy every detail of their life together. He never tired of watching her with her birds and often would bring up worms from the "worm barrel" in the cellar for her to feed them. Their congeniality was apparent to all their friends. "To see you together was a lesson in the beauty of love," Harold Laski wrote to the Justice.

Next to his wife, Justice Brandeis was probably the person closest to Holmes during most of the Washington years. They lived only a little more than a block apart and often walked or rode or sat in the park together, talking "to get the wrinkles out a little." Besides the satisfying intellectual companionship, there was also a sort of spiritual kinship between the two men. Each treasured the friendship. "Brandeis is a great comfort and help to me," Holmes once told Laski.

Brandeis occasionally twitted Holmes with his lack of knowledge of current situations and problems. Once Holmes wrote to Pollock: "Brandeis drove a harpoon into my midriff with reference to my summer occupation. He said you talk about improving your mind; you only exercise it on the subjects with which you are familiar. Why don't you try something new, study some domain of fact? Take up the textile industry in Massachusetts and after reading the reports sufficiently, you can go to Lawrence and get a notion of how it really is. I hate facts."

When Brandeis persisted, Holmes told him to send a box of books to Beverly Farms to be included in the summer's reading. The box arrived and was opened. One look at the ponderous studies of the textile industry, employers' liability, the eight-hour day, and so on was enough for Justice Holmes. After a moment of real dismay he made one of his quick decisions. "Just nail it up and send it back," he told the man who had opened the box. Then, with a sigh of relief, he went back to reading Plato.

Some critics felt that Holmes should have tried to acquire more knowledge about industrial and economic subjects. Others felt that his very remoteness from politics and practical matters made him better able to interpret the Constitution, "to see the particular in the light of the universal." He tried "to exhibit some hint of horizons even in small details" and "to see the application of the broadest rules." Through this philosophical approach difficulties often could be solved more wisely and on a longer-term basis.

Holmes's searching mind was always trying to

open windows on life. "I am impressed and depressed at the narrowness of the sphere within which
I reach and the worlds of which I know little more
than that they exist," he wrote Einstein. He admitted feeling a "duty to seek self improvement,"
which he thought might after all be a better occupation than trying to improve one's neighbor.

"I want to produce as long as I can," he said again
and again, but what he produced must be first rate,
and he watched himself constantly to see that there
was no falling off in his work. He bragged that he
"sneaked a base" and turned seventy-seven "without
too much noise," and he admitted that now his goal
was to work until he was eighty. "If I reach that (in a
little over two years)" he wrote Einstein, "no doubt
I shall fix another time to be climbed to." And with
a touch reminiscent of his poet father he added, "I
made this poem to myself as I walked a few days
ago.

> I will sit in the seats of the mighty
> If I can, until I am eighty (pronounce *îty*)
>   And what I'll do then
>   In the following ten
> I leave to the Lord God Almighty."

1 2

The Great Dissenter

JUST BEFORE his eightieth birthday Justice Holmes wrote to Harold Laski, "Writing opinions seems to me quite as easy as it ever was and I think I write better English." Even after all his years as a judge, he admitted that every week he was frightened when he first tackled the cases assigned to him, "but always when you walk up to the lion and lay hold the hide comes off and the same old donkey of a question of law is underneath."

The Justice was much pleased by a book, *Collected Legal Papers,* which Laski had compiled of Justice Holmes's most important writings in the field of law. He wrote Laski, "I am glad to gather up this little basketful before my eightieth birthday, as I was glad to get out *The Common Law* before my fortieth."

Like that earlier book, the *Collected Legal Papers* brought high praise, both in the United States and in England. It pleased Holmes that reviewers spoke of the strength and matchless style of its words and of the immense legal knowledge and keen insight on which they were based. In answer to the comment of Morris Cohen, noted philosophy professor, that it was "concrete realization of the author's contention that to think great thoughts one must have a heroic soul," Holmes immediately wrote Cohen, "Well, I expect a fall soon, for I begin today proud — very proud of such words from a philosopher whom I so deeply respect."

The justice had rather expected his wife to provide something a little special to celebrate his eightieth birthday. She had spoiled him that way for years, but this time she seemed to think it would be enough, on the Sunday immediately preceding the big day, just to go out to dine, as they often did on a Sunday evening. She did suggest that they dress in honor of the occasion, so the Justice put on his white tie and tails and she donned her best gray satin. She seemed slow, and he grew restless, but at last the two of them went down the long stairs together.

As they paused at the foot, the folding doors into the dining room opened, lights went on, and more than a score of male voices rang out in a glad "Happy Birthday, Justice!"

The Justice crossed the small middle room and

paused at the threshold of the dining room. He shaded his eyes against the blaze of lights, then exclaimed, "Ghosts!" as he recognized first one, then another of his former secretaries. "I knew she was up to something," he murmured shakily.

He walked around the long table, lovely with spring flowers and gleaming crystal and silver, and shook hands with each man. "Chain gang!" he called them collectively, but, "Son," he said to each one individually, in a voice that trembled with emotion.

"Mrs. Holmes fixed it all," one of them said. "She made us come in through the kitchen," another added. And a third exaggerated, "We've been waiting for hours."

It was a party that neither the Justice nor his wife nor any one of "Holmes's Annuals" present ever forgot. When the feasting and the toasting were over, they called for a speech from the Justice. Afterward, none of them could recall precisely what he said, but all remembered the note of affection in his voice and his parting admonition to "stick to the rugged course."

In writing to Laski about the party the Justice called it "a most affectionate, wholly delightful meeting, and it melted my heart."

The newspapers and news magazines made quite a bit of the Justice's entering on another decade. "As he turns the corner of eighty," the *New York Times* commented, "the road stretches away again, and ambition to go farther returns." The Justice remarked that when a man becomes eighty the press begins to consider him interesting. But the newspaper "puffs," as he called them, added to the reviews on his book, pleased and encouraged him. He wrote to Laski, "That book, coupled perhaps with my birthday last March, has brought out such a set of notices that I feel my life has had its reward — the only one I care for — in the assurance from those voices I value that I have more or less done what I desired but did not dare to expect." And he exclaimed, "Altogether I have been at the top of the tree!"

When Chief Justice White died, many hoped that President Harding would make Justice Holmes the Supreme Court's Chief Justice. He was its oldest, its best known, its most learned, and certainly its most beloved member. After twenty years as an Associate Justice, to be made Chief Justice would have been the culminating glory of Holmes's life and would have meant much to him personally. But the Justice knew, as the President knew, that the responsibility was a heavy one for a man in his eighties, even a man with Justice Holmes's remarkable vitality. No one could foresee that he would outlive William Howard Taft, who was appointed to the high post, by several years.

Some of Justice Holmes's most important opinions were written in his eighties. Even he was satisfied with them and knew that they were good. "I gather from the brethren that they are pleased," he wrote Laski, adding modestly, "I can't see that my work has fallen off."

His opinions were, in fact, written with such freshness and strength that Roscoe Pound, dean of the Harvard Law School, wrote to Harold Laski, "I have just been reading a new batch of Holmes's decisions. If I read them as nameless productions I should ask what newly vigorous mind has been added to the Court."

At eighty-three, Justice Holmes was awarded the Theodore Roosevelt Medal "for distinguished service in the development of public law." The citation stated that he had "shown a breadth of humanity and an understanding of essential human rights." In his acceptance, Justice Holmes said that for a brief time the award had made the dream of his life — "to accomplish an intellectual achievement" — seem a reality.

Justice Holmes was much disturbed by some of the things he saw around him in this postwar period. Many Americans, enjoying unparalleled prosperity, had become fat and complacent, ultranationalistic and intolerant. They were suspicious of any opinion that differed from their own and they applauded the courts' repressive judgments and harsh sentences on dissenters. Holmes saw this attitude as a threat to the Constitution and to the country. He preferred, he said, "the risks of tolerance to the dangers of tyranny."

When the Supreme Court upheld the decision which affirmed the right of the Postmaster General to forbid a newspaper to use the mails because of its socialistic leanings, Justice Holmes dissented. "The use of the mails is about as much a part of free speech as the right to use our tongues," he declared, and he warned people of the need for "keeping open the channels of free, though heretical, inquiry."

He dissented again in the Gitlow case in 1925. This concerned a small group of radicals who had written and distributed a pamphlet which the majority of the Supreme Court decided was an incitement to action to overthrow the Government by force. Justice Holmes held in his dissent that their "left-wing Manifesto" presented no active danger to the Government. What was really on trial, he said, was the right to air unpopular theories, and again he pleaded that all ideas be given their chance. Freedom of speech, he wrote to a friend, was being reduced to "you may say what you choose if you don't shock *me*."

Justice Holmes disliked dissenting from his brethren and it was distasteful to him to be called the Great Dissenter. "I dislike even the traditional *'Holmes Dissenting,'* " he wrote to Laski. "We are giving our views on a question of law, not fighting with another cock." But views could be more freely expressed in a dissent than in a watered-down majority opinion, and when Justice Holmes felt it his duty to speak up, as in matters of the protection of individuals under the First Amendment, he did so, courageously, courteously, and firmly.

"I have been somewhat active in dissent," he wrote his friend Einstein, "which I regret, but regret more the position of the Court on some important questions." After all, the Supreme Court was not a club of learned elderly gentlemen. It was a vital part of the American Government, set up to interpret the country's laws according to the Constitution, and the American people had a right to expect every Justice to give to it his best and most honest thinking.

Justice Holmes's powerfully worded dissents and his excellently written majority opinions were capturing the attention of the American people and making them more conscious of their Supreme Court and its place in the national life. Because of Justice Holmes they read about its sessions with greater interest, and more of them came to see the Court in action. They came, partly at least, to catch a glimpse of its most distinguished member and to pointed him out, saying proudly, "There's Holmes, and there are all the other judges."

"I had always thought," Judge Holmes joked, "that when I got to be fourscore I could wrap up my life in a scroll, tie a pink ribbon around it, put it away in a drawer and go around doing the things I wanted to do. But I learned that when you have taken one trench there is always a new firing line beyond."

In 1927, when he was eighty-five, the Justice celebrated his twenty-fifth year on the Supreme Court and his forty-fifth year as a judge. When he denied the rumors that he was about to retire, the American people were pleased. Most of them did not realize that he was, in a sense, working for his country without pay, since the pension he was entitled to would equal his salary. They felt merely that for Justice Holmes to leave the Court would be a great loss to the nation. In her *Yankee from Olympus*, Catherine Drinker Bowen quotes the newspapers as saying at this time that the Court could ill spare a man so much younger than his brethren in mind and spirit, and one newspaper as editorializing: "His opinions have such freshness, his mind is so penetrating and in tune with the age and his general view of life has such tang and piquancy that we hope he will stay right where he is as long as his powers permit."

That, according to all indications, might be for some time. The summer after he was eighty-one the Justice had had an operation from which he slowly but completely recovered. Before going back into the Washington house Mrs. Holmes had insisted on having an elevator installed to save her husband from climbing the long flights of stairs. But sometimes she would hear him coming up the steps because he forgot — or disdained — to use the new device. He usually rode to work now, and often Justice Brandeis and he drove home together, talking about many things and thoroughly enjoying each other's companionship.

Drives increasingly took the place of walks, with Charley the coachman now driving an automobile, though for shorter rides the Justice and his wife still used the "old buggy and horse that we have employed since before automobiles won," the Justice wrote a friend. On longer drives they might follow the "noble Potomac" up to its scenic Great Falls, or ride up the Maryland side of the river, cross on the Chain Bridge, and return on the Virginia side. At the zoo, which they still visited frequently, they would stroll about, stopping to admire the baby animals, laugh at the antics of the monkeys, look in on their old four-footed friends, and marvel at the buzzards "wheeling nobly high overhead." They also attended some formal affairs, such as a White

House garden party, a flower show, and the opening of the Freer Gallery of Art.

Spring continued to be the Holmeses' favorite season, and they did not have to go far to enjoy it. "In my back yard," the Justice wrote his friend Pollock, "'there was first a magnolia with a mass of flowers, then a double flowering apple tree — a mass of pink — now a wistaria hanging the adjoining wall with purple blossoms."

After the spring came the joy of escape from the Washington heat and the retreat northward to the old brown house perched upon a rock beside the sea. The Holmeses never tired of this north-of-Boston region. Nearly every day they drove about Cape Ann, usually now by car, to see and enjoy "the cliffs, the beaches, the old towns, and the occasional old Yankees."

They visited old houses in Newburyport and Marblehead, and in Marblehead "zigzagged through its old streets and visited its old burying ground at the top of everything with a wonderful outlook on the sea." One afternoon they went to nearby Gallows Hill where they were told by a young boy who offered his services as a guide, "they hanged the witches." Mrs. Holmes invited the lad to "hop in," and when he confided to them his ambition to go to Harvard College and Law School he got from them, said the Justice, "five dollars and our blessing."

When Salem was three hundred years old, Justice and Mrs. Holmes drove over for the celebration. A young man, recognizing them, rushed to get chairs, which he put in the best place for them to see the procession "celebrating the town *now* and *then.*"

One day they went to Plum Island and "sat on the white beach stretching out of sight, with the black-blue ocean illimitably in front and a few mackerel gulls zigzagging swiftly overhead — infinite space and air," the Justice wrote Einstein.

They rarely went out in the evening, but once they attended an opera performance in an outdoor theater in the woods, and another evening went to a carillon concert in Gloucester.

In 1925, when both were eighty-four, the Justice wrote Einstein, "Our latest adventure was going to a County Fair, seeing the horses, hearing the fakers all about, buying popcorn, and my wife professing to have been cruelly stopped by me from mounting a horse on a merry-go-round."

The Justice claimed he had "idled" through the summer weeks in order to "jump into work rested." But vacation was never completely idle, for there was much correspondence to attend to as well as the great sacks of certiorari. Whether in Beverly Farms or Washington, Justice Holmes had a horror of doing less than his share of the work of the Court, and he never did. He kept a sharp eye out for fear the Chief Justice might ease up on his assignments, but he saw no sign of this. "If my work is not as good as ever," he wrote to Pollack, "I don't care to prolong it." And to Laski, "The work comes as easy as ever, but physical exertion is more difficult and limited." Though at eighty-seven he wrote Dr. Wu, a talented young Chinese law student, then teacher, "I still feel so much of the zest of life."

It was not the Justice but his wife who showed the first signs of failing health. In her eighties, though she stood as straight as ever, Fanny Holmes moved more slowly and tired more easily. The summer she was eighty-eight she relinquished the tending of her Beverly Farms flowers to others and contented herself with merely watching her roses burst into rich bloom. The motor rides were shorter now, and the overnight and luncheon guests fewer.

Back in Washington, Mrs. Holmes went out less and spent more time in her upstairs sitting room. "My wife had a tumble which left her very uncomfortable just after recovering from a long and trying pulldown that I suppose was the grippe. But no serious harm was done," the Justice wrote his friend Einstein. He was wrong. Mrs. Holmes had broken her hip. She suffered silently, and at the end of April, 1929, she quietly died. Because of her husband's service in the Civil War more than half a century before, the burial was in the Arlington National Cemetery, just across the Potomac.

Justice Holmes wrote a friend that his wife's death took away "a half of my life." But he showed the stamina of his New England forebears and of his own stalwart philosophy by going about his work as usual, attending the Court sessions and conferences and continuing to write his share of opinions. In his reply to a letter from Lewis Einstein which recalled "the real warmth of her [Mrs. Holmes's] heart which she did her best to hide" and her "true generosity in her sympathy with those who needed it," the Justice said that it was better that his wife should die than live on in pain. "I think, too," he wrote, "that it was better that she die before I do; she was the same age as I, and I think would have been more at a loss than I am if left alone." To Sir Frederick Pollock he wrote much the same thing, adding, "We have had our share. For sixty years she made life poetry for me."

At this time there was a case before the Court which troubled the Justice deeply. An intelligent middle-aged Quaker lady had been denied citizenship because she was a pacifist. The majority of the Court went along with this decision of a lower court, but Justice Holmes dissented. Within a month of his wife's death he stood up in the Court and delivered his last and perhaps most famous "free-speech" dissent.

"If there is any principle of the Constitution that more imperatively calls for attachment than any other," he declared, "it is the principle of free thought — not free thought for those who agree with us but freedom for the thought that we hate." He believed that at stake was not the idea of whether Rosika Schwimmer would or would not bear arms in case of war, but her devotion to the Quaker teachings against the principle of war. Should she, he asked, be penalized for her belief in the teachings of the Sermon on the Mount?

Twenty years later the law caught up with Justice Holmes's thinking in this matter, and for the words "the will to bear arms" substituted "the will to perform work of national importance."

Another noteworthy Holmes dissent had come a year earlier when the Supreme Court decided that it was lawful for the Government to secure evidence by tapping telephone wires. In his dissent Holmes called wiretapping "dirty business" and said he thought it "less evil that some criminal should escape than that the Government should play an ignoble part." As so often happened, Justice Brandeis agreed with his opinion, but it was Justice Holmes who wrote and delivered the dissent.

Chief Justice Taft thought that Justice Brandeis

had too much influence over his good friend Justice Holmes. It was high time, the Chief Justice thought, for "the old gentleman" to retire. But Holmes had something else in mind. "If I should reach ninety in harness, I would consider it an achievement," he said. He admitted that "the little burdens were heavier as one nears ninety," yet at Beverly Farms that summer after his wife's death he and his secretary had gone over more than two hundred certiorari and he had stood for a full-length portrait for the new student reading room at Harvard Law School. It was painted by Charles Hopkinson who had, said Holmes, a gift for catching a likeness and for vividness. The following summer, on a flying visit to Cambridge, he had the satisfaction of seeing the portrait hanging beside that of John Marshall, and, said the Justice, "It pleased me mightily."

That year of 1930, when Chief Justice Taft became seriously ill, it was Justice Holmes who took his place. During Taft's illness and until another Chief Justice was appointed after Taft's death, the eighty-nine-year-old Justice presided faultlessly and with seeming ease over the sessions of the Supreme Court and over its Saturday conferences. In the seventies he had said, "Eighty is old." Now he stated with equal conviction, "It seems as if a man must reach ninety to be really old."

Charles Evans Hughes, appointed to succeed

Supreme Court of the United States in 1930
Left to right, front row: Justices McReynolds and Holmes; Chief Justice Hughes; Justices Van Devanter and Brandeis. *Rear row:* Justices Stone, Sutherland, Butler and Roberts

William Howard Taft as Chief Justice, wondered about the ability of so old a man as Justice Holmes to fulfill his responsibility on the Court. He watched as the Justice took notes while the lawyers spoke, and during the lunch recess on some pretense asked if he might look at them. To his satisfaction he saw that the aged Justice's notes were concise, clear, and absolutely to the point.

In another widely noted dissent Justice Holmes disagreed with the majority of the Court in their decision against the tax-levying power of a state. It was, he said, "cutting down what I believe to be the constitutional rights of the states." Although he did not as a rule like publicity, Justice Holmes was not displeased when a newspaper ran a picture of him delivering his opinion, with a one-word caption below it: ALERT.

13

The Finishing Canter

THE YEAR ROLLED AROUND to another birthday —
Holmes's ninetieth. He was still in harness at the
goal he had set for himself. On that Sunday of
March 8, 1931, the nation celebrated the birthday of
the beloved Justice — the oldest ever to sit on its
highest Court. There were flowers, letters, and
messages from everywhere. The March *Harvard
Law Review* was made up of articles about him
written by the world's most respected and learned
men in the field of law. So was a new book, entitled
Mr. Justice Holmes. These things made him dare to
hope that he had realized his dream — not for
"place or power or popularity" but "the trembling
hope that one has come close to an ideal."

That evening a large audience gathered in Cambridge to pay tribute to Harvard's most illustrious
living alumnus; to one who, as the historian Charles
Beard put it, "commands our minds by the power of

Portrait of Justice Holmes by Eben F. Comins

his thought and our hearts by the magic of a good life." The mood was one of affection as well as esteem. "We honor him," said Chief Justice Hughes, "but what is more, we love him." The speeches were broadcast and were tuned in to the study at 1720 I Street, Washington, where a microphone had been installed so that Justice Holmes might say a few words at the end of the program.

They were few, for the Justice said, "to express one's feelings as the end draws near is too intimate a task." But they were memorable. He compared the last years of life to a race with its little finishing canter. One did not stop work, for "the work is never done while the power to work remains."

After his little speech the Justice sat quietly beside the study fireplace, eyes closed, wrapped in thought. The few close friends who were with him — among them Harold Laski, who told the story — hesitated to interrupt the silence. Suddenly the Justice chuckled; his face lighted up with the old impish smile, his eyes flashed, and he said, "I wish that my father could have listened tonight!"

Writing a friend about the birthday the Justice said, "There were some touching things happened . . . I found myself feeling more than I expected."

The next noon Justice Holmes appeared as usual in his place on the bench beside the Chief Justice.

He quoted Emerson, " 'It is time to be old,' " then said, "But I don't feel so today."

Day after day he went to Court, missing his wife constantly but trying not to show it or to let it affect his work. Sometimes when he closed his eyes while listening to lawyers presenting cases before the Court people were sure he was napping. Yet he seemed never to miss the important points.

Soon after his ninetieth birthday a group of Justice Holmes's ex-secretaries paid him an affectionate call and asked him to pose for a second portrait by Hopkinson. This one was to be a half-length one, which they planned to present to the nation to be hung in the handsome new United States Supreme Court building soon to replace the historic old room in the Capitol. The Justice was pleased with their request and agreed to pose for the portrait. He admitted however that, like many of the older Justices, he had little interest in the new building. "We have done some pretty good business in the old place," he said.

That summer at Beverly Farms, with the help of his secretary, Justice Holmes examined about one hundred and fifty certiorari. He read and was read to — "sleeping when I saw fit," he confessed. He took short motor rides, had callers and a few luncheon guests, and in the evening played his usual game of solitaire. His friends did not allow him to be lonely — "hardly as much as I wish," he said. Lengthy conversations tired him, and he was really thankful when left alone to read, write, and be read to. Yet he thoroughly enjoyed the visit Sir Frederick and Lady Pollock paid him. The old friends had much good talk, and each morning the two aged gentlemen took "a short slow toddle" together.

The Justice's household employees were devoted to him. "I have some angels for servants," he wrote Lewis Einstein, "and they look after me with a care that makes me very comfortable." Mary, the house-keeper who had been with the Holmes household for many years, was the soul of kindness and con-sideration. The Justice called her a dictator, "who seems to think it is a wrong to her if I do anything for myself."

After posing for the second Hopkinson portrait Justice Holmes sat for a bust by a Russian sculptor. "Both picture and bust seem to me very successful," he wrote Einstein, "except that I fear the bust flattering."

That fall the Justice did his work with a kind of disciplined determination, putting into his opinions even "more gusto than the average." His philoso-pher friend Morris Cohen said that he had never seen the spirit of man defy time so chivalrously. But the Justice's friends noticed that he stooped as he walked from his home to the waiting car and from the car to the Supreme Court chamber in the Capitol, and he acknowledged feeling "flabby" and tiring easily.

Early in 1932, the Justice one day found it difficult to read the majority opinion it was his duty to deliver in Court. His voice was weak and uncertain; he stumbled over the familiar words. At the end of the Court session he stopped by the clerk's desk. "I won't be in tomorrow," he said briefly.

That evening Justice Holmes sent his resignation to President Hoover. "I bow to the inevitable," he wrote, and in graceful words he expressed his gratitude for the many kindnesses of the President and of his brethren.

The next day the Justice received by special messenger a note from those brethren. It began: "Dear Justice Holmes: We cannot permit your long association in the work of the Court to end without expressing our keen sense of loss and our warm affection." It went on to comment on the exceptional quality of his long service. "Your profound learning and philosophic outlook have found expression in opinions which have become classic, enriching the literature of the law as well as its substance." The note mentioned his personal charm, his independent spirit, and his kindly and generous nature, and concluded by expressing the hope that "relieved of the burden which had become too heavy — you may have a renewal of vigor and that you may find satisfaction in your abundant resources of intellectual enjoyment." To this note the Chief Justice and the seven remaining Associate Justices affixed their names, declaring themselves, "Affectionately yours."

Justice Holmes answered the note at once. "My Dear Brethren," he began, "You must let me call you so once more. Your more than kind, your generous, letter touches me to the bottom of my heart." And he ended, "I shall treasure it as adding gold to the sunset."

Newspapers and news magazines gave much space to Justice Holmes's resignation. The oldest Justice ever to sit on the Supreme Court, he had been a member of the Court for more than a fifth of its history and had helped make more than a third of its decisions. Not a single newsman would disagree with Felix Frankfurter's words: "He was probably the greatest mind and the most complete human personality we have had on the Court." Or with Owen Wister's estimate: "The most illustrious and beloved figure ever on the Court; a great personage in its history."

Friends as well as journalists urged Justice Holmes to write his memoirs now that he had the time. But the Justice saw no need of doing this. He had put the best of himself into his work as a jurist, and he intended to follow the precept he had once laid down: "Part of the greatness of a great life . . . consists in leaving it unadvertised." In accord with this feeling he destroyed many personal documents.

It was not hard for the Justice to fill his days. "Old age and routine make time fly fast," he wrote Laski. "A daily drive, a daily nap, a daily walk, and solitaire every evening leave not too much time for improvement." His secretary read to him by the hour. Though some books were chosen with a view to "improving the mind," the selection also included "a copious allowance of murder stories." One can almost hear the Justice chuckle as he wrote Laski, "I mean to have some good out of being old."

There were callers — many of them. Justice Holmes was still good company — the best in Washington, Chief Justice Hughes said. He made his visitors chuckle, he made them think, and he gave many of them an altogether new outlook on old age. The Chief Justice remarked thoughtfully, "If this man, so brave and wise, so old yet so youthful, finds life so good, you think to yourself, it must be good." And a journalist wrote: "With all the weight of his learning, he is one of the gayest, wittiest, most charming men alive. His life should dispel the foolish idea that thought is dull."

Summer at Beverly Farms brought even more

callers. The Justice was pleased that they included so many young people. "The young men of today seem to me to be a better lot than when I was young," he commented, and he made the keen observation that much of their energy, which had formerly produced literature, was now going into science. He listened attentively to their definitely expressed opinions and answered their serious questions thoughtfully. "I won't refrain from talking about anything because you're too young," he told a sixteen-year-old caller, "if you won't because I'm too old." But the Justice was not old; he was "inescapably young," as Harold Laski said. "None of us who love him feel that he is old," said Laski, "only that he is more experienced than we are."

It annoyed Justice Holmes that one of his great pleasures, that of letterwriting, was becoming increasingly difficult for him. Now that he had more time to exchange ideas and experiences with congenial distant friends it was most irritating to find that the effort was almost too much for him. His handwriting, he admitted, had grown "small and uncertain," for no reason he could see but old age. "The body is an awkward drag on the mind," he confessed. Then he quickly added, "I am still interested in life and shouldn't mind an extra piece."

The Justice was surprised when Felix Frankfurter insisted on sending him as usual a new secretary the fall after his retirement. Objecting only a little, the Justice welcomed the twenty-eighth of the "Annuals." The young man became an almost constant companion — a mail-opener and answerer, a book-and-pamphlet sorter and librarian, a receiver of callers and messages, and a reader-aloud for hours at a time. He soon learned not to stop when the white head began to nod and the gray-blue eyes to close, for as surely as he did, he would hear a soft voice inquiring, "Well, Sonny?"

The secretary also took care of Justice Holmes's personal finances, for the Justice hated figures. "My Heavenly Father never meant me to do sums," he said. One day, while preparing the Justice's tax return, the secretary asked conversationally, "Mr. Justice, don't you hate to pay taxes?" "No, young feller," came the quick reply, "I *like* to pay taxes. With them I buy civilization." Never in his life, the Justice said, had he questioned anything to do with pay for his services. "I have been too happy to do the work."

It was the secretary who had the honor of greeting the new President of the United States, Franklin Delano Roosevelt, when he made an unprecedented call on Justice Holmes only a few days after his inauguration.

Picking up the open book whose reading his call

had obviously interrupted, the President asked, "Why do you read Plato, Mr. Justice?"

"To improve my mind, Mr. President," the Justice replied without hesitation.

After a conversation which ranged from deep-sea fishing to prizefighting, President Roosevelt earnestly asked Justice Holmes for his advice. The Justice, although he liked to brag about not reading the papers, was well aware that the nation was in a desperate economic situation. He was silent a moment, then answered solemnly, "Mr. President, you are in a war. I was in a war once too. And in a war there is only one thing to do — Form your battalions and fight."

For two more years the Justice lived on, enjoying his "extra piece" of life. He became less and less active, living ever more simply, yet continuing to relish the beauties of nature and contact with challenging ideas, both through his friends and through books. "There is so much to learn," he sighed.

Driving out on a raw late-winter day — perhaps looking for signs of his favorite season — the Justice caught a cold which developed into pneumonia. His nephew, brother Ned's only son and director of the Boston Museum of Fine Arts, came down from Boston, as did Felix Frankfurter and two of the Justice's ex-secretaries. They helped the current secretary receive messages and calls from friends whose concern impelled them to make frequent inquiries. Of these, Louis Brandeis stopped at the 1720 I Street house most often; other callers included Chief Justice Hughes and Mrs. Franklin Roosevelt. Upstairs the Justice joked feebly with his nurses. He called the oxygen tent "a lot of damn foolery," and smiled gently at the few who were admitted to his bedside. His breathing grew heavier and, early in the morning of March sixth, ceased.

It was on his ninety-fourth birthday, March 8, 1935, that the Justice was buried beside his wife Fanny in Arlington Cemetery. The Supreme Court Justices were his pallbearers; the Army sounded taps, the President standing at attention.

Tributes poured in from all over the world. The papers reminded the American people of the impact Justice Oliver Wendell Holmes had made on the nation's life, and of the effect his opinions had had on the laws of the land. They referred to his stirring speeches, particularly those in defense of freedom of speech and the press and of the free exchange of ideas. They also informed the people that Justice Holmes had left half of his money, without strings and without explanation, to the United States of America.

The American people were fully conscious of Justice Holmes's long and significant contribution to the nation in the realm of ideas and were grateful for it. But what they liked best to remember about him was his glowing, human, noble personality. Felix Frankfurter expressed this in the words he wrote to Lewis Einstein soon after the Justice's death: "He died as he lived with unflinching gayety and rectitude. And nothing that will ever be written or said of him will testify to his quality more than the strange deep discernment of the whole nation that the country's finest figure had departed. . . . The quality of him somehow or other broke through to let all the millions who could not even remotely put into words his significance feel his glory as part of their own."

And so it has remained and so it will continue to remain. Oliver Wendell Holmes's words of wisdom are still quoted, his opinions are still cited, his decisions are still followed, his remarkable personality is still admired. And it is quite safe to predict that his influence will persist and that, in his own words describing the power of the thinker, "a hundred years after he is dead . . . men who never heard of him will be moving to the measure of his thought."

Other Books by and about Justice Holmes

Bent, Silas. *Justice Oliver Wendell Holmes*. New York: Vanguard, 1932.

Bowen, Catherine Drinker. *Yankee from Olympus*. Boston: Little, Brown, 1944.

Holmes, Oliver Wendell. *The Common Law*. Boston: Little, Brown, 1881, 1923.

———. *The Occasional Speeches of Justice Oliver Wendell Holmes*. Compiled by Mark DeWolfe Howe. Cambridge: Harvard University Press, 1962.

———. *Touched with Fire: Civil War Letters and Diary of Oliver Wendell Holmes, Jr., 1861–1864*. Edited by Mark DeWolfe Howe. Cambridge: Harvard University Press, 1946.

———. *Correspondence of Mr. Justice Holmes and Lewis Einstein, 1903–1935*. Edited by James Bishop Peabody. New York: St. Martin's Press, 1964.

———. *The Correspondence of Mr. Justice Holmes and Harold J. Laski, 1916–1935*. Edited by Mark DeWolfe Howe. Cambridge: Harvard University Press, 1953. 2 vols.

―――. *The Correspondence of Oliver Wendell Holmes, Jr., and Frederick Pollock, 1874–1932*. Edited by Mark DeWolfe Howe. Cambridge: Harvard University Press, 1941. 2 vols.

Howe, Mark De Wolfe. *Justice Holmes: The Proving Years, 1870–1882*. Cambridge: Harvard University Press, 1963.

―――. *Justice Holmes: The Shaping Years, 1841–1870*. Cambridge: Harvard University Press, 1957.

Judson, Clara Ingram. *Mr. Justice Holmes*. Chicago: Follett, 1956.

Lavery, Emmet. *The Magnificent Yankee: A Play in Three Acts*. New York: French, 1945, 1946.

Marke, Julius J., ed. *The Holmes Reader*. Dobbs Ferry, N.Y.: Oceana, 1955, 1964.

Acknowledgment

I AM GLAD that Justice Holmes enjoyed writing letters and that he wrote so many of them. His letters to Pollock, Laski, Einstein, James, Wu, Cohen, and other friends are so delightful and so revealing of the man that I have used them frequently, though briefly, in this book. For most of them I am indebted to those collections of correspondence mentioned in the list of books at the conclusion of this biography; the others were found in various periodicals.

My thanks go also to the staffs of the Ferguson Library of Stamford, Connecticut, the New York Public Library, and the venerable Boston Athenaeum.

The Author

Index